The Concept of Organization

BLACKIE BOOKS ON ORGANIZATIONAL ANALYSIS

The Concept of Organization
The Hospital: An Organizational Analysis
The School: An Organizational Analysis
The University: An Organizational Analysis

The Concept of Organization

An Introduction to Organizations

David Bradley and Roy Wilkie

BLACKIE: Glasgow and London

0 216 89693 2 (Paperback)
0 216 89694 0 (Hardback)

Blackie and Son Limited
Bishopbriggs, Glasgow G64 2NZ
5 Fitzhardinge Street, London W1H 0DL

Filmset and printed by Thomson Litho, East Kilbride, Scotland.

Contents

Introduction

This book is an introduction to organizations. It arises out of our interest in the subject, particularly since 1967 when we began to work together in the Department of Administration at the University of Strathclyde. One of us spent the next five years in charge of the Department, the other, along with three or four others, was a lecturer in the Department. During that time we were responsible for a three-year Ordinary degree course and a four-year Honours course in Administration, for students in the Schools of Business and Administration and Arts and Social Studies. New classes were constructed, prepared and taught in what were called Basic Administration, Structural Theories in Administration, Organizational Behaviour, Contemporary Organization Theory, Organization of Innovation, Bureaucracy, Advanced Organizational Behaviour and Advanced Organization Theory. The numbers of our students in each of these five years averaged 350, the majority of them attending the first-year Basic Class.

These classes were all new. Unlike philosophy, economics or politics where one can examine the experience of other universities in the preparation of their syllabi and curricula, the classes we were responsible for had to be argued from first principles. Both of us read, thought, talked and taught about organizations as teachers and researchers over these years. Consequently the problems we examine in this book are ones we have lived with for some time. Our colleagues and ourselves had graduated from a number of disciplines—philosophy, politics, sociology, economics and law. We all shared a professional interest in the study of organizations, but our particular interests and approaches to the subject varied considerably. We all shared some notions about education. We were agreed that teaching was an important activity and that our primary obligation was to our students. We also disagreed on many matters.

Some of us saw certain limitations to the study of organizations as an undergraduate principal subject. Others hoped that in time the emphasis of the Department would move from undergraduate teaching to postgraduate instruction. One or two wanted the direction of development to be towards professional training courses for administrators. We all had different opinions about the status of organizational analysis and how progress should be achieved. However, whatever our views on the subject matter, in one respect we were identical. We were all members of the same Department, teaching according to the same degree regulations, and in the same university. Now, in the first chapter, we draw an analogy between taking on an organizational role and being tattooed. While one of the many pleasures of being an academic is the freedom one has to choose one's tattoos, the fact is that working together for many years in the same organization has left us bearing certain marks in common. In the same organizational situation, facing the same set of problems and having to work out co-operatively and act upon the same practical solutions, it could not be otherwise.

One of these marks relates to the present state of knowledge and thinking about organizations. We found, for instance, that introductory texts to the study of organizations too often resembled potboilers, the scissors and paste efforts of academics meeting publishers' demands to cater for a fast growing market. Often such efforts were completely derivative. One recent introduction, on its first page, refers to three major nineteenth century social theorists (none of whom are mentioned in the bibliography) and at no point in the text refers directly to an actual organization or organizational event. Other books seem to address two audiences at once, the beginner and the advanced student. Potted summaries of the major writers are supplied— usually a redundant exercise for advanced students—while at the same time critiques of these are given which can only be properly appreciated if more than a potted version of their work is known, something that beginners will not have.

We are fairly confident that we have made mistakes in this book, but we hope that most of these derive from our attempt to write a truly introductory text. The adverb is deliberately added because we have set out to discuss some of the key problems of organizations without either the benefit or hindrance of referring to the work of other organization theorists. Clearly we have been unable to avoid coming into contact and sometimes conflict with the ideas of others. What we did not want was to obscure actual thinking with fulsome bibliographic references and extensive quotations. We have aimed at clarity at the expense of overqualification. This fault, we hope, will be rectified by the reader himself, for, if he is stimulated to pursue the study of organizations further, the main purpose of such an introduction will have been served.

Two final points. One: this book presages a series of monographs which will be concerned with presenting an organizational perspective on one organization at a time. It is intended that the comprehensive school, the university, the merchant ship and the hospital should be among the early publications in this series. The extent of the series will depend on the response which the first ones receive. We would be glad to hear of other possibilities for the series, either from students of organizations who would like to present one organization themselves or from those who would like to suggest a need which they would like someone else to fill.

Two: we owe a number of debts which we want to acknowledge publicly. During these five years, Sir Maurice Dean, who is a Visiting Professor to the Department, was a great friend and support. Then there are our students, researchers and teaching colleagues, who in diverse ways contributed towards our learning and enjoyment during these years. We owe a special debt to Hugh Livingstone, Nick Perry, and Ann Rosengard, critical colleagues and good friends. A special word of thanks is due to Stephen Bennett who read most of the manuscript and to Robert Rae who read it in its entirety. Both of them gave us many valuable criticisms. We had the greatest secretary in Patricia McTaggart, whose work in the Department generally, and on our script in particular, continuously threw serious doubt on our belief that no one in an organization is indispensable. Lastly, we want to thank our wives, Jan and Jill, and the children, Jacqueline, Lauren, Sean, Joanna, Catriona, Moya and Abigail, without whose continual, but nevertheless welcome, interruptions, this book might have been completed months ago.

CHAPTER 1

The Study of Organizations

There are many reasons for studying organizations. In the first instance some organizations are very powerful. They shape events in ways which have critical consequences for people's lives. When an organization announces that one of its aims in the next decade is to reduce drastically the number of people it employs as, for example, the British Steel Corporation has just done at the time of writing, at least one important consequence will be that many thousands of human beings will be forced out of the steel industry to seek employment in other occupations, in other industries. The loss of a job is usually a harrowing personal experience. When it occurs on a large scale as the direct result of the deliberate strategy of a single organization it becomes a matter of public concern.

Ways in which the interests of organizations produce traumatic peaks and depressions in the private lives of individuals are presented to us daily by the public media almost as a matter of course. The fate of an organization such as Upper Clyde Ship-builders *receives* a great deal of attention and *becomes* the subject of great controversy. Very many similar but smaller matters remain unreported, yet each one, for some people, somewhere, is likely to be a dominant fact of life. As sources of employment, organizations enter into the lives of most people, but, of course, there are many other points of entry. Not just the fact of employment but also the characteristics of the job provided and all that they mean for the human being involved are the products of forces which result from, and are finally shaped by, decisions made in the organization. For most of us, our work lives are organizational lives, but as consumers, we are also, to a great extent, organizationally shaped. How much we can consume is usually a function of financial returns from our work in organizations. What we can consume—the type, quality and quantity of goods and services—may not be completely determined by factors controlled by organizations, but it is organizations that make most of the critical decisions about our consumption. Other examples of the power of organizations may be drawn from such fields as education, health, religion, and, of course, politics.

Organizational power is often demonstrated in a dramatic and public way. What sorts of things contribute to the successful generation and exercise of power by organizations? What kinds of power do they have? Are there other kinds of power? We ought to concern ourselves with the nature and extent of organizational power. Can organizations do what they please? Or are there rules which regulate organizational acts? If so, how closely do they underpin and shape organizational power? Who makes them? If organizations fail to abide by the rules, what follows in the way of sanctions against them? What means are available for challenging organizational decisions? What are the conditions which allow for the effective criticism of organizations?

These questions focus attention on the accountability of organizations. Taking organizations to task for what they do is often a problematic business. In cases where these actions are questioned by an individual, the response of the organization concerned will be of great interest to the student of organizations. For instance, when a young American lawyer criticized a motor-car-producing corporation for its deliberate evasion of car safety measures, one response of the organization was to try to uncover discreditable aspects of his private life. One of the aims of a democratic political process is to constrain the ability of interest-groups to act on their own behalf without due consideration for the interests of others. The study of organizations would provide systematically collected information about organizational aims, the procedures through which they create their policies, the managerial processes through which they are implemented, the consequences of such activities, both direct and intended, indirect and unintended. The importance of this aspect of the study of organizations cannot be exaggerated. Our lives are more and more affected by the accumulating side-effects of organizational actions, as well as by direct actions themselves.

There are a great many questions one would want to ask about this. How desirable is it to involve all the people in the organization in the decision-making process? If it is desirable, what procedures will be needed to make such involvement effective?

To what extent should an organization be statutorily bound to take into account the interests of others when it acts? When the organization concerned is a governmental body, consensus on the principle of democratic control seems to exist. Non-governmental organizations which are, nevertheless, very powerful, and in some cases wealthier than the nation states within whose boundaries they operate, should no less be the object of democratic scrutiny.

The first point we made suggested that organizations do have considerable power to shape the situations people live and work in. A second reason for studying organizations is that organizations shape people's behaviour in a more direct fashion. There are two important ways in which they do this. First of all, people, as employees or members of organizations, do not act in a private capacity but more or less in conformity with the requirements of their organizational positions. They obey orders, comply with rules, and fulfil obligations. We would want to know how much discretion individuals have in their organizational roles. Under what conditions, for example, can they be blamed for obeying orders?

It will be important to find out, for example, how people become members of organizations. How much of a choice is their membership? Sometimes people are dragged into organizations and become captives. Sometimes they queue to enter. But not all organizations are like prison camps and golf clubs. In some cases the situation is quite cloudy. For example, universities are often described as voluntary organizations. No one is forced to join them. Yet it is sometimes the case that a student may enter university and not feel that he is 'volunteering' his services in the way that a person might when he joins a political party. He may believe that he must go to university in order to achieve some important aim in life, such as a good career, social status, or the happiness of his parents. The actual activities he will be required to engage in as a student may not be very attractive to him. He may feel more like a captive of 'the system' than a willing member of an academic community. The university, like other organizations, will have made arrangements to affect the member's behaviour, and these arrangements will be based on assumptions partly drawn from some notion as to why the person became a member in the first place. The nature of these arrangements, the assumptions upon which they are based, and the actual degree to which they affect the behaviour of organizational members will be important matters for the student of organizations to examine. But, at first sight, it may be difficult to discern how one student differs from another student with a radically different motivation.

The second way in which organizations shape people's behaviour is less obvious. Human beings have knowledge, hold opinions, possess beliefs and ascribe to values. To the extent that our world is one of organizations, then they will be important sources of that knowledge and those beliefs. Individuals will tend to be the sort of people they are through the experience they acquire in and of organizations. Sometimes, of course, organizations deliberately set out to 'shape the man'. Organizations such as schools, universities, psychiatric hospitals and churches are sometimes called 'people-changing' organizations, their main aim being to alter the behaviour of their members. Other organizations, while not intending to obtain more than an outward conformity from their members, nevertheless influence or mark their general ways of behaving. It is this permanent effect on the way people are, whether deliberate or not, which is of importance to the student of organizations. We are all familiar with examples of the ways in which people become characteristically affected through their association with particular types of organizations. The army officer may act more like a soldier towards his family than as a husband and father. It has not been unknown for a defending lawyer in a murder case to plead mitigation for his client by claiming that he committed the act in part because he had been trained to kill by the army. The long service spinster schoolteacher, whose dominant life experience has been confined to the classroom, may unwittingly treat all sorts of people and not just school pupils, as if they were children. The former convict may relate to all authorities in the same way as he related to the prison staff. It seems, then, that taking on organizational roles, whether voluntarily or not, may be more like being tattooed than putting on an overcoat. The one is more difficult to take off than the other.

If organizations do largely inform our attitudes and values and hence our behaviour generally—either directly through the requirements of an organizational role or in some more pervasive fashion—there is a strong case for a careful examination of how this comes about. How does an organization affect the behaviour of its members? If it is meaningful to talk of the behaviour of students and civil servants, miners and seamen, as if they had had their behaviour shaped by universities, the Civil Service, coal mines and ships, in what ways has this come about? Are there significant variations within the behaviour of such groups of people? If there is, why is this so?

These last illustrations lead us to yet another link in the set of reasons for studying organizations. An outstanding characteristic of our sort of society is the number and variety of complicated and large-scale tasks in which organizations are engaged. We can very easily take this fact so much for granted as to ignore its importance. In John Steinbeck's novel, *The Grapes of Wrath,* a farmer and his family are threatened with eviction. They attempt to discover and shoot whoever is responsible for the eviction order. Gradually the farmer realizes his fate is being decided by something other than human beings. People can be shot; banks and financial institutions are something different. This passage is echoed in the Arthur Penn film, *Bonnie and Clyde,* where Clyde hands his gun to an evicted farmer who fires at the house he has just been evicted from and at the eviction notice outside it. The bank isn't hurt, but he enjoys it. These examples illustrate the power of organizations as well as the frightening impersonality of their activities. They also show men who, as farmers in the impoverished mid-West America of the thirties, led lives of which the familiar ingredients were the soil, weather, family, neighbours, and friends, that is, until they were caught up by events far beyond their control, and often their understanding. They contrast interestingly with life in a modern British farming community, as portrayed in the BBC radio series, *The Archers.* For the Archers and their neighbours, organizations such as the agricultural ministries, banks, finance corporations, County Councils and marketing boards are familiar, if not altogether welcome, factors in their existence. Our society, we are told, is an organizational society, and this is largely true. (Man is born free yet is everywhere in organizations.) It would therefore be a travesty of our claim to build up knowledge of ourselves and of our society, if we spent a lot of time and money studying, say, the social variation of eating haggis and drinking malt whisky among fishermen of North East Scotland, and studied none of the effects that organizations are having on our lives. The fact that we are a society of organizations must have implications for our society, and for us as students of society.

This fact usually introduces academic books about organizations but it now appears as the basis for a number of popular books, as well as cinema, radio, and television programmes. The books have tended to offer advice and guidance to young people about how to advance their careers within the organization. Television, cinema and radio have placed dramatic serials and dramatic series within organizations. The various power games that are played out at the top of the organization by different kinds of troubleshooters have turned out to be successful audience-pullers. One such television series of six programmes broadcast at peak viewing-time on a Sunday night was, in fact, simply called *The Organization*. Where books, for example, are in such demand that their sales run into hundreds of thousands, we can safely assume that they must be being bought to fulfil some need. Such books are shaped by, and in turn shape, society and we find it of more than mere sociological interest that, by the end of the sixties and beginning of the seventies, the notion of 'the organization' had become a common reference point in popular culture.

A fourth reason for studying organizations stems from the fact that all organizations are in some sense managed. At least some positions in an organization are managerial in function. People who occupy these positions are supposed to be concerned about the activities of the organization as a whole. This concern is usually directed towards creating a more problem-free and less costly organization which will be more effective in achieving its ends. By virtue of their organizational jobs, it is claimed that managers will be in particularly advantageous positions from which to study organizations. The advantages of looking at them from the bottom up could equally be argued. From the top, though, they can more easily provide access to others to study organizations on their behalf. It is not surprising that, especially with regard to privately-owned firms, the most powerful encouragement for the study of organizations has come from managers of organizations. As a means by which some managerial problems may be eased or solved, the study of organizations has greatly developed in recent years, both within and outside universities. It is fairly usual to cite study for managerial purposes as the 'practical' reason among other (sometimes called 'pure') reasons for examining organizations. Following this practice, this would be the fourth but only 'really practical' reason we have mentioned so far. We are reluctant to agree with this. To do so would be to imply that only managerially-motivated organizational study is 'practical' or 'useful'. This is certainly not the case. As we have tried to show, organizations, and the practice of management inherent to them, have consequences of a most immediate, important and practical nature for all of us, and coping with these consequences must be an immediate, important and practical activity.

It would, therefore, be more accurate and helpful to refer to this fourth reason as the 'managerial' rather than the 'practical' one. It is the case that the degree of success of an organization will in some part be a product of the type and quality of the behaviour of people occupying positions in the organization. Managers will want to understand the behaviour of people as members of their organization, particularly in order to find out whether any of the significant causes of their behaviour can be usefully altered to produce more favourable outcomes for the organization. It is, of course, quite feasible to imagine a greater understanding leading to the conclusion that no useful alteration can be made by them. This might be for more than one reason. For example, a problem of high staff-turnover might possibly be solved through paying higher wages, but the firm may not be able to afford to pay these because it would drastically alter their competitive situation. A matter of economics has blocked off one possible solution. Moral reasons may also be important. Prison escapes could conceivably be stopped altogether if the prison authorities kept their captives in a very undernourished and weak physical state. Perhaps giving a one hundred pounds reward for each examination hurdle successfully overcome might reduce student failure rates (and indirectly put an intolerable burden on university car parks), but this has not been put forward as a serious proposition. In other words there are a great many constraints, if not actual prohibitions, on the application by managers of knowledge about human behaviour. Not the least of these may be the resistance and power of those managed.

Managers are interested in two broad aspects of behaviour—

types of organizational behaviour and the quality of its performance. First, what *types* of activities will be conducive to the organization's greater success? The study of organizations may allow for the evaluation of different types of activities and so lead to the inclusion or growth of some types and the exclusion or reduction of others. For instance, should theatres engage professional experts in marketing? If they do not have enough seats for all the people who want them, more seats may be the answer. If, as is more likely, they could do with vast increases in the number of their paying customers, the answer might be a qualified yes. It would be qualified because paying a marketing expert to boost audience attendance has to be costed against other possible ways of spending the money—for example, buying in better actors or directors, and so making the theatre's product more attractive. Whether or not the best answer is given will then depend upon information gathered by studying theatre organizations.

The second managerially-motivated question will concern the ways in which people perform such activities. In our theatre example, deciding to create a marketing post is one thing; recruiting somebody to the post and ensuring that someone performs it according to directions and standards laid down by the organization is another. The effective performance of the job will depend upon the skills of the person recruited and the degree of enthusiasm he has for exercising those skills. This enthusiasm will depend upon such matters as pay and the status and importance accredited to the jobholder. It will also depend upon how the job is integrated into the rest of the organization (for instance, will the marketing officer be under the direct supervision of a theatre manager, artistic director, or the board of management?), how much of the organizational resources will be allocated to marketing, and, by no means least, to what extent the theatre acts on the information and advice given by the marketing officer. Desirable standards of performance, whether from car-workers, actors, prisoners or priests, do not automatically follow from the decision by managers to specify that certain activities will take place. The general point is the same. Whether or not such standards will be reached will depend upon a variety of circumstances, some of which, in varying degrees, will be amenable to control through managerial action. Moral, political, legal, economic, and technical considerations will inform such action; as also will considerations about just what it is the organization is trying to achieve.

It would be easy to go on drawing attention to features and problems of organizations that repay enquiry and study. Perhaps no thinking person requires to be convinced of the importance of such study. What might be much more contentious as an issue is the claim that this study is in some way a worthy subject for pursuit in universities. Arguing that organizations are important subjects for study is one thing, claiming that special conditions of an intellectual or social nature ought to support their study is another. For a start, does organizational study not already take place in university departments under the aegis of a variety of developed disciplines? The first reason we gave for organizational study—the power of organizations and the conditions under which that power is exercised—appears to be at least part of what we mean by politics. Surely the study of organizations for such reasons will be undertaken by political theorists and scientists? The second reason we gave was that organizations shape people's behaviour. Isn't this the subject of inquiry of psychologists and sociologists? Again, the fourth reason— organizational study for managerial purposes—isn't this an activity already engaged upon by students of business, economics, public and social administration, all of which have places in existing departments in universities? It would seem that in so far as organizations constitute a subject-matter worthy of serious academic study, then serious political scientists, psychologists, sociologists and administrative experts will already be engaged in this activity. What room could there possibly be for a special breed of 'organization' experts?

There are two answers to this question, the first of which involves an argument about ways of describing and analysing organizations, the second an argument about the usefulness of making organizations generally a 'strategic site' for the raising and discussing of critical questions, the answers to which are not provided by any single one of the more conventional disciplines in universities. First, one can argue for the usefulness of developing a distinct, systematic and precise vocabulary of organization. This vocabulary will be useful to the extent that it helps us to describe, analyse and understand those features and problems of organizations we are interested in. The history of the study of organizations consist of a variety of more or less successful attempts to create such a vocabulary. Some attempts may be seen to be connected with each other and patterns of development of a distinctive language of organization may be traced. These patterns are the various 'schools of thought' of organizational study. A description and appraisal of the more important ones constitute the subject matter of most introductory textbooks on organizations. A number of texts are little more than rapid tours of the works of various writers, written by somewhat less than cheerful guides. Others take on the task of unravelling complex issues over the 'scientific' status of various claimants to the title 'theory of organizations'. The problem here is that many 'theories' of organization usually lay claim to too much: they desire to replace the conventional disciplines of politics, sociology and psychology,—from this view 'all is organization'. Or they appear to imagine that, as the subject matter of 'theories of organization' is organizations, they have a monopoly-right to study all organizations; the other disciplines can have the remainder. Now, if you take organizations out of the remit of these other disciplines, a great deal of their subject matter will disappear. What would the study of politics look like without the study of particular organizations? The confusion here is the supposition that there are activities going on in society which are 'economic', 'social', 'political', 'religious' and so on, and other activities which are 'organizational'. This is clearly absurd. The point about our sort of society is that a great deal of its activities are carried out in and through organizations, and in situations, organizational or otherwise, which are affected by organizations. Organizations are discrete, empirical units of action in our society. The better the language we have for understanding them the better will be the success of any discipline which aims to contribute more knowledge and understanding about our society. For any one who finds organizations as part of his subject of study, and who shares a concern for the reasons we have just been discussing, a way of talking about organizations will be necessary.

A second response to the claim for making the study of organizations a discrete activity rests on the problems raised by the complexity of societies, particularly fully-fledged 'organizational' ones. More often than not, serious issues and problems raised about life in such societies do not fall neatly into any particular one of the present disciplines within the social sciences. For instance, the enslavement, torturing and killing of many European people by the Germans during the last war was a fact of appalling significance and importance. It did not come about as a result of a single type of activity which may be labelled 'political', 'ideological', 'military', 'economic' or 'technological'. Understanding its significance and importance, explaining why it could happen, coming to grips with an assessment of its consequences, simply cannot be achieved within any single discipline of the social sciences. Very valuable contributions may be made by various specialist disciplines but, at some point, a study of the facts of the 'Final Solution' which has the breadth necessary to grasp fully its importance to us as human beings must possess a focal point which they lack. The cutting edge of organizational analysis might be that it can provide one such focal point. History would be another. The history of events leading up to the 'Final Solution' is a history of organizational acts, of people acting in, and on behalf of, organizations, and of people attempting to resist organizations. In seeking out responsibility for these crimes, we come across names and positions—Hitler, Himmler, Sturmabteilung, Schutzstaffel, Einsatzgruppen, particular concentration-camp commanders. Any answer will include an organizational answer.

A multi-disciplinary study of such issues as a conjunction of each particular discipline's analysis would be insufficient. The activities central to these issues are predominantly complex organizational ones. A vocabulary of organizations should allow for a fuller grasp of this complexity as well as for the inclusion of relevant, conventional disciplinary studies. Finally, what we would regard as the satisfactory means for dealing with such issues in universities will not occur spontaneously, given the present pattern of social science disciplines. They must be *organized* and this means teachers, students, resources and organizational studies curricula. Whether or not independent departments should be created as expressions of this educational concern is an issue to be argued out within the organization of the university.

CHAPTER 2

The Contexts of Organizations

Recently, a group of workers, wanting better working conditions and more pay, went on strike. During the course of the strike they demonstrated in the streets of their town, and were subjected to baton charges, dog attacks and high pressure water jets. Eventually their leaders were arrested and gaoled, and the strike was broken through the mass dismissal of the work force and the recruitment of other men prepared to work under the old conditions. The employing organization was a company of international standing. Technologically it was similar to other organizations of its kind throughout the world. Also, it operated to make a profit, and its managerial structure was of a familiar bureaucratic pattern. Its response to the workers' demands for a better deal predictably was one of resistance. To have acceded to them would have meant increases in the costs of production, a loss of competitive edge, and probably less profits. In terms of its goals, technology, administrative structure, and the conflict of interests between management and workers, it was a typical capitalist industrial organization. The firm, however, was in South Africa, the workers black South Africans. Consequently, the nature of the strike, and its meaning for the firm and for the workers, were radically different from what it would have been if it had occurred in a similar organization in Britain.

This example is intended to illustrate the point that societies differ in ways which may have important consequences for the nature and activities of organizations within them. Where an organization is located is important. Countries differ in their political systems, wealth and its distribution among the population, science and technology, type of communications media, educational systems, the general stock of beliefs and ways of behaving, and the art and culture of their people. These differences will be expressed in part through variations in the types and distribution of organizations within each country. As the example of the South African organization (which happened to be a part of a British company) demonstrates that, even when organizations are similar in terms of their formal structure, goals, technology and economic characteristics, in other important respects they may still differ considerably.

Perhaps the most critical source for some of these differences is the political environment of organizations. British firms with plants in South Africa are unable to run them in exactly the manner they would in Britain. South African laws prevent them. Some organizational positions may only lawfully be filled by individuals with a specified skin colouring. The management of South African firms cannot negotiate with the independent representatives of their employees because the independent association of workers for such purposes is illegal. Strikes, too, are proscribed by law.

In some countries, governments may do other than inhibit the ways in which employees pursue their interests in organizations. They may legislate to alter the administrative structure of industrial organizations to ensure worker-participation at all levels of decision-making. Alternatively, all commercial and industrial organizations may legally form part of the state bureaucracy. Whatever the case, all organizations are affected by, and will be expected to pay heed to, the political and legislative actions of the state. We said in Chapter One that taking organizations to task for what they do can often be a problematical business. Governments, through the political and legal order they maintain, can help or hinder in this task. The modern study of organizations has taken root in democratic societies, in which receiving answers rather than asking questions is often the most difficult problem. Ralph Nader, harassed by the big corporation he dared to criticize, did have successful recourse in the law. The danger, however, is that the study of organizations may take for granted the political freedom to ask questions about its subject matter. Such complacency may extend to the point where the influence of the political order on organizations is neglected altogether. Then, certain key organizational features, for instance goals, technology or administrative structures, may be treated as inherent and fixed—the immutable essence of organization—rather than seen to be what they are, the historical consequences of the ways in which certain men choose to act in particular situations. In totalitarian states we may be sure that men do not make the mistake of ignoring the political environment of organizations. Generally, in such states, the political apparatus permeates and controls the administrative structures of all major organizations, whether their goals are to do with sport, art, education or industry.

Perhaps our complacency arises because the study of organizations has been largely confined to industrial enterprises. These operate in situations relatively free from direct government control, and under-pinned by the ideology of free enterprise operating in free competitive markets. Not surprisingly, it is only when public organizations have been studied that any great awareness and concern for their political environments has occurred. An example of this is the well-known study of the Tennessee Valley Authority, an organization created as part of the New Deal programme in pre-war America. This case study was outstanding, not least because it examined issues concerning the democratic control of the organization, the interests, rights and obligations of groups and organizations affected by its operations, and the attempts that were made to resolve these problems.

In Britain, there exists a large number and variety of public organizations created or taken over by successive governments. The nature of their relationships with Government and Civil Service varies considerably—some, for instance, are legally charged to provide a subsidized service to the public, others to act as self-funding profitable concerns. Many of these organizations possess a legally defined independence from direct governmental and political influence. The British Broadcasting Corporation, the universities, police forces, hospitals and the various Sport and Art Councils are examples of such organizations. How independent of governmental control these organizations actually are is sometimes difficult to assess. Their relations with government are usually hidden from public view, and guesses about their nature are liable to be based on inferences about the social and educational backgrounds of the people appointed to run them by government, rather than on an examination of their legal charters.

Generalizations about such organizations are usually difficult to make without reliable information about the influence of their political environment. When they are possible without such information, they tend not to be about the most important aspects of their functioning. For example, it is probably true to say that television and radio broadcasting organizations everywhere share certain organizational features. They will be alike in technology and in the types of technical and professional personnel they employ as broadcasters, directors, electronics engineers and so on. They will all use artists, performers, actors and authors. However, their goals, expressed in terms of the form and content of the programmes they broadcast, and the views and information they disseminate, vary enormously. They may all claim to broadcast in order to entertain, inform and educate, but these broad and abstract terms can and do cover a multitude of different things. What they actually cover in any particular broadcasting organization will have a great deal to do with the role permitted it by the state.

For example, the British Broadcasting Corporation is reliant upon Parliament for its right to broadcast. During the twenties and thirties the BBC managed to develop as an organization remote from government interference, certainly not as a branch of the civil service which radio broadcasting has become in some countries, for example, O.R.T.F. in France. Sometimes the Government has actively attempted to influence the work of the BBC, and sometimes it has succeeded. "Assuming the BBC is for the people, and that the government is for the people, it follows that the BBC must be for the government in this crisis too", wrote the Director-General at the time of the General Strike—which, at least, is an interesting set of assumptions. But over the years the independence of the BBC from government control has become a part of the way of life in British society. Yet the government has the right to appoint the Chairman and other governors of the BBC, which would suggest either that the organization would be sensitive about its relation to government policies or that the government-appointed governors would ensure that the organization did not stray too far from these policies. This is not to deny that the BBC can and does resist strong attempts by government to adopt a party line—in 1956, the Suez crisis prompted one such attempt, and the BBC stood its own independent ground—only that this independence is too valuable to be taken for granted. Broadcasting organizations may be born with independence but it is by no means a necessary condition of their birth or life thereafter.

Not only the government of the day makes up the political

environment of the BBC. There is also the official Opposition which, for example, with the government, decides the right of any smaller party to be allocated time on the air during election periods. At the 1959 General Election the Conservative and Labour parties were allocated 95 minutes each, with the Liberal Party receiving 25 minutes and the Scottish and Welsh Nationalist Parties being denied any air space. In the United States, political parties are denied time on the air only if they cannot afford to pay for it.

Opposition parties are as eager at times as governments to interfere with the BBC, particularly of course when they believe they have been unfairly represented by the Corporation. In 1970 the British Labour Party, which had just become the official Opposition, protested to the BBC over the showing of a television programme called *Yesterday's Men*. The Governors of the BBC had seen the programme before it went out, and had no other mechanism to review the Labour Party's protest but themselves. The defence was the judge and jury. The hullabaloo that resulted led to the setting up of a Complaints Commission of three worthy gentlemen who have the right to adjudicate over matters of controversy in broadcasting programmes, so that the net outcome is a reduced role for the Board of Governors.

In a few years' time the charter of the BBC is due to expire. It is possible that a full scale enquiry into broadcasting in all its aspects will be undertaken. The total reorganization, even dismemberment, of the BBC is a possibility. Whatever changes may occur, they will have to be authorised by Parliament.

Its relations with particular governments, and with potential ones, constitutes the most persistent and critical environmental fact of life for the BBC. That this is so is no accident. The BBC, together with other organizations that make up the mass communications media, itself is a major environmental influence on all organizations in our society, governments included. The legally guaranteed freedom to publish and disseminate information and opinions about the activities of the powerful is a remarkable stimulant to the development of sensitivity to their environments by organizations. The press conference, or the threat of one, is one of the few influential weapons that an individual may wield in the face of the big batteries of the large-scale organization. The independence of organizations such as the BBC from the control of political parties and corporate interests is a vital condition for such influence. The dependence of newspapers for their existence on advertising revenue from large industrial concerns is a nagging reminder of how fragile is the maintenance of this guaranteed freedom in practice. The manipulation of public opinion through the media is a professional activity on which large sums are spent by all kinds of big organizations in our society.

In the next chapter, one of the subjects we examine is the notion of the legitimacy of an organization's goals and activities, how well they are received and thought of by various groups of people. A great many references to this notion are contained in the literature on organizations. Yet, despite its obvious connections with the ways in which opinion and information are carried through the mass media, few studies have systematically included an examination of the influence of this aspect of their environments on the nature and activities of organizations. There have been, however, plenty of books and manuals written to advise managers on how to exploit the media in order to create favourable opinion about their organizations' public images. Any study of organizations which neglects the importance of the structure and control of the systems of communication in society runs the risk of being not a little naive.

The political order and mass media are important environmental influences on organizations. They are also the means through which they may influence their environments. The basic elements through which politics, communications and organizations have to work are the beliefs, opinions, judgements, interests and life styles of the population. There are many aspects of organizations that are incomprehensible unless we pay particular attention to the social and cultural characteristics of people. People bring their environments with them into their organization. People are rarely, if ever, wholly creatures of particular organizations: organizational selection procedures, recruitment policies, wages and salary structures and other control mechanisms, are responses to the problems created by this fact.

In the earlier example, the management of the firm in South Africa were legally bound to act in relation to their employee in ways that would have been illegal, if nothing else, in Britain. However, their management-worker relations would not only be different because of the law. They would also have to take into account that their workers were illiterate, politically-deprived members of a systematically exploited class in South Africa. For these workers, the beliefs and customs of their tribes would still be important sources of the way in which they viewed the world. They would also have come to expect, and be more or less accustomed to, particular ways of relating to white people, particularly white people in influential positions. Harsh authoritarian supervision, by British standards if not by the standards of other African countries, will usually tend to be built into the structures of firms in harsh authoritarian states, no matter how underpinned it is by a paternalistic racist ideology. Consequently, the British management of the plant in South Africa might find that methods of supervision developed, for example, in a factory in Sheffield, or on the campus of Harvard Business School, may cut very little ice when it comes to managing a brewery in Johannesburg.

One might imagine that it is unexceptional to point to the possible importance of this sort of environmental influence, but, as we said earlier, the ignoring or playing down of such influence frequently mars any worthwhile analysis of organizations. A good example of this would be from the early writers on management, who assumed that there would be one best way of managing any organization. They extracted from business firms what they considered were the main managerial activities—planning, evaluating, and the like—and claimed that these activities ought to be capable of being established on certain 'principles'. These principles might be 'one man, one boss', or the number of people any one manager can actually manage.

Having established the essential principles of managing, these writers maintained that basically all organizations would be managed in the same way. The trick is in the persuasive 'basically', for it, like its cousins 'ultimately', 'in the long run', 'really', 'truly', usually operates to direct your attention away from prominent characteristics of the situation you are facing, and towards some other characteristic which may be relatively unimportant. The belief that there must be 'one best way' of managing an organization is monstrous enough, but it can perhaps most easily be exposed by recalling the problems that managers in this country usually voice when they are put in charge of a labour force of another country. And not just in South

Africa. During the Second World War, it was common currency in the British Armed Forces that you could not manage Indians 'for love nor money'. American managers in Scotland have been appalled at attitudes to their work held by Scotsmen. In other words, ideas of management established in one environment have come unstuck when practised in another.

Another example of this way of thinking which ignores the importance of the social and cultural environment to the detriment of sound analysis, was in the assessments made of the Chinese Communist Party in the fifties and early sixties by Western writers. If the criteria for a Communist totalitarian government were an all-embracing ideology, a monopoly of political power, arms and a centrally-controlled economy, then China, satisfying these criteria, was a totalitarian country. Dissatisfied by this fairly humdrum conclusion, Western commentators went on to assert that China was nothing but another version of Stalinism, with the (often unspoken) implication that they had mistakenly supposed the Chinese Communist Party to be something different. The Stalinist model was a familiar one at the time, with a well-known family of expressions, concepts and images, a definite range of references and a well-defined starting point for speculation.

Of course, the application of the Stalinist model to China has some basis in fact. There were enough similarities between the Soviet Union and China—for example, in the use of Five-Year Plans, the economic ministries, the planning mechanisms, the structure, functions and aims of the Communist Party—to suggest other parallels. Nor was there anything necessarily vicious in approaching the subject of Communist China with the question—to what extent do actual explanations of what is going on in China approximate to the structure of the Stalinist model? The dangers were, however, that more would sometimes be read into specific events than they could bear, and that important features that were there would pass unnoticed. The emergence of the Chinese Communist Party as *de facto* controller of China by 1949 was described by some as a seizure of power with the direct aid of the international Communist movement, rather than the victory of a fairly popular army led by a determined group of men accepting, in the well-known tradition of Chinese history, the mandate of heaven which the Kuomintang had absolutely spurned. Again: the character of the Chinese Communist Party has been drawn in terms of Stalinist and anti-Stalinist elements, continually locking in struggles for control of the party machine, but the schisms and purges that have taken place within the Chinese Communist Party have been of a radically different nature to those of the Soviet Party. The Chinese opted for massive 're-education' and the cultural revolution, the Russians for fabricated charges, faked trials, and physical elimination. Again: the simple facts of pest control, litterless streets and fanatical cleanliness were put down to intensive brain-washing, ignoring the fact that social persuasion, the eliciting of social response by exhortation and precept, had traditionally been part of Chinese government.

What we are trying to draw out is the relevance of the cultural and social environment within which the Chinese Communist Party established itself as the ruling party within China. That it imported European political ideas is unquestionable. That it has considerably modified them is often unrecognised. Yet, to a serious student of politics, much analysis of the Chinese Communist Party would be impotent if it ignored Chinese history and culture. The reasons why most predictions of its behaviour since 1949 have gone awry are also due to this neglect.

Often an organization's main environmental factor is another organization or group of organizations. The BBC is acutely aware of the existence of a rival television broadcasting system. Scientists from universities regularly scan the announcements of awards from research councils to see if another university is stealing a march on them in some research field. It used to be a standard joke in social scientist circles to work out the kinship pattern of the members of the awarding committees and the recipient academics.

Of course, this aspect of environmental importance has long been appreciated in business. Most firms are aware that their environment is largely composed of other firms. In the furniture and timber industry, for example, there are over 4,000 firms within the United Kingdom, some of which will be concerned with a specific product, say, the manufacturing of billiard tables, while others will be in direct competition with each other over the sale of beds, tables and chairs. Such competition theoretically helps to keep down the prices of these goods. If the products are homogeneous, if there are a large number of firms, if there is free entry and exit from the market, then the spread of information about these factors should ensure that a buyer will only purchase from the cheapest seller. The conditional clauses do not pertain just like that, but the furniture firms in this country tend to approximate towards some of the conditions of perfect competition. Furniture firm managers often visit the showrooms of other furniture firms.

The furniture manufacturers clearly do not visit their competitors in order to buy furniture. They do so in order to pursue more effectively their organization's goals. Similarly motivated visits or communication with other organizations by the officials of various public organizations seem to be less a matter of course than they are in private industry. For example, the radical restructuring of the National Health Service which is at the moment taking place, has been undertaken primarily because proper relationships between its constituent organizations have failed to develop. Relationships between prison authorities, probationary and welfare agencies and other organizations concerned with helping discharged prisoners to pick up their lives again, were and are frequently more characterised by feelings of mutual hostility rather than co-operation. A similar situation exists in the field of mental health. Recently we heard from a social worker that one of her clients, a young mentally ill girl, had twice been discharged from a mental hospital without the hospital authorities contacting and informing the relevant social work department. We were told that this was by no means an unusual situation. Yet both mental hospital and social work departments are organizations working towards similar ends, often treating the same people. Their relationships with each other will have a marked influence on their effectiveness. A study of either organization would have to take this fact of their environments into account.

What we have argued is that no organization is an island; that, if we are to explain why one organization has developed one way rather than another, then we must look at such things as the legal, political, social, cultural and organizational environments within which the organization has its place. Of course, it is sometimes difficult to locate these environmental factors and to assess their weight in the shaping or determining of the organization. It is difficult, if not practically impossible, to describe Niagara Falls in physical terms, but such difficulty would not negate systematic enquiries into its water flows, water composition and the like.

A clear illustration of the need to consider the complex influence of the environment on the nature and activities of an organization, and the impact on its environment that an organization may have, is to be found in the recent well-publicized events that overtook one of Britain's largest shipbuilding firms. Intertwined into this organization's affairs were political, governmental, economic and social influences and happenings, all of them reported and interpreted by the various media organizations. The organization in question is the Upper Clyde Shipbuilders— U.C.S.—a business firm formed during the sixties as a result of the Geddes Report on the general state of British shipbuilding, which was either receiving too few orders in bad times or incurring heavy losses in the full-order-book, boom times. A Shipbuilding Industry Board was set up, partly to encourage rationalization of the industry through mergers, and the U.C.S. was formed from a number of shipbuilding firms at the upper part of the River Clyde in Scotland. The Shipbuilding Industry Board gave the U.C.S. £12 million, the government of the day gave it another £9·5 million, but by 1970 the U.C.S. went bankrupt and has since cost the government another £11 million— making up over £33 million from the government, or the taxpayer, depending on how you emphasise these matters. Moreover, the government was a major shareholder in U.C.S., holding 49% of the share capital, which, in turn, tended to foster the notion that, no matter how dire the straits Upper Clyde Shipbuilders might manage to arrive at, it had a shareholder who would always be financially capable of bailing it out. The government was not only an important funding element in the environment, it was also involved in the determination of the management of the firm. At the time, it was a fashionable idea that shipbuilding management should have experience in other industries and not, as in the past, be drawn wholly from shipbuilding experiences. The first chairman of U.C.S. was previously a director of Thomas Tilling, a hosiery manufacturing firm. The government went along with, and actively encouraged, this idea.

The bankruptcy of the firm in 1970, however, did. not end government influence. Although the government refused to put more money into the firm, thus precipitating the crisis, there were still questions of economic and social policy that could only be answered by government action. What alternative employment was the government going to provide for the 8,000 men who worked in the firm? What about the thousands of other workers in the dependent supply companies? What were going to be the social consequences of this unemployment? What was the human cost of unemployment? It was, and still is, part of the government's responsibility, to tackle these questions. And since the liquidation of U.C.S. the government has spent a great deal of time and money trying to attract potential buyers to salvage the remains of the large consortium. Not the least of the reasons for their anxiety to salvage the pieces of U.C.S. was the active concern of the U.C.S. workers, of the various members of Parliament, together with the television, radio and press coverage, with the implications that closure would have on the whole Clydeside community. When the liquidation was announced, the workers of the firm decided to stay at their work, to participate in a 'work-in', with the demand for the 'right to work' and no redundancies. Support for this drastic action came from a number of trade unions and social groups. Money was collected throughout Britain and from abroad to alleviate the difficulties, while the workers' representatives spent a great deal of time consulting and negotiating with various organizations over the issue of the survival of the company. Political parties of the country were also involved, and there was clear evidence of the major ones being split, not only along ideological lines, but also along nationalist ones as well. For weeks and months the mass media kept the problem in the public's view. Not an unimportant factor in the way in which the U.C.S. problem was eventually resolved was the skill with which the workers' leaders used the press and television.

As the U.C.S. case and all the other examples we have used in this chapter indicate, organizational analysis will have to pay attention to the environments of organizations, and the nature of the relationships that organizations have with them, if it is to avoid being incomplete or parochial in the understanding it gives us of their nature and activities. In the next few chapters we will be looking at concepts that provide, as it were, eyeball-to-eyeball confrontation with organizations. This chapter has served, we hope, to avoid the ever-present risk of myopia in such a venture.

CHAPTER 3

Organizational Goals

Organizations, it may be said, have a life of their own. We speak of such-and-such a company laying off men, or of a university appointing a new professor, or of a hospital building a new intensive care unit. The words 'company', 'hospital', 'university' are clearly a condensed or abbreviated way of describing a whole series of activities that result in men being made unemployed, a new professor being appointed, and patients being better looked after. To appoint the new professor, for example, a clerk in the university might have had to write a letter to a number of newspapers and journals requesting the insertion of an advertisement. On the receipt of applications, someone—perhaps the same clerk—will have to write to the referees. The Vice-Chancellor or a committee will look over the applications and prepare a short list of candidates. Invitations will be sent out and then the candidates will be interviewed. One candidate will be recommended to the appropriate body of people for ratification, and later an announcement will be made that the university has appointed professor X to the chair of Y. Such an account briefly suggests the lines along which the sentence which ascribed activity to the university should be unpacked, but, of course, in normal discourse such unpacking is rarely necessary. Most people know full well what we mean when we refer to the University of Strathclyde, the British Broadcasting Corporation and Imperial Chemical Industries.

This means that these names are conventional shorthand ways of describing simple as well as complex activities of people. Of course, not all activities of people in an organization can be accurately described as activities of the organization. The same clerk who placed the advertisement in the newspapers may be trying to date his superior's secretary and hence may spend a lot of time in her office talking with her. It would be amusing, but misleading, to claim that the University was trying to date the girl. Similarly, if he uses his telephone to make a personal call, it would be wrong to hold that this is another activity of the organization. And, if there is an agreement made during the morning coffee break that a number of his colleagues should accompany him to the Cup Final on Saturday, such more complicated activity could still not be called the activity of the university. In other words, it is only those actions of the individuals in the organization which have been authorized, or at some time might be, that can properly be described as the organization's actions.

How are people authorized? We should be aware that authority in an organization can take different shapes, but the authority usually associated with organizations is the authority that particular jobs and positions carry with them in the organization. Sometimes called formal, positional or *de jure* authority, it usually means the authority that an occupant of an office or position in the organization has, which gives him the right to give orders and make certain kinds of decisions. When people are authorised to have authority in this sense, then we can say that they represent the organization, sometimes even that they are the organization. "L'etat, c'est moi", Louis XIV is supposed to have said, and many a managing director or Vice-Chancellor has presumably envied his total blending of the job and the organization. As is often said of bosses on the Clyde, they walk about as if they were anointed, instead of appointed.

On the whole, then, organizations have a life of their own when people take up duties that such positions prescribe. The organization is committed to appointing the professor once the secretary of the appropriate university committee is authorized to write to him inviting him to accept the vacant post. If the successful candidate accepts, then the university is committed to a whole series of activities, providing him with accommodation and equipment as well as paying him a salary. Moreover, if, when he arrives to take up his appointment, he finds that the particular clerk who sent out the advertisement, the members of the committee who interviewed him, and the Vice-Chancellor, have all left, retired or died, the university will still be committed to providing him with his promised conditions of employment. To be authorized can mean committing resources beyond the actual life or work expectancy of an occupant in an office. The organization can then be usefully defined by the extent of its formal authority system. What the offices of the organization authorize, the extent of the powers and the rights, the amount of resources that are available for committal, are all indicators of what kind of an organization it is that we are examining. All of these, however, can only make sense if we know what the organization is trying to do.

Surprisingly, it is much more difficult to tie down the goals of an organization than one would normally assume. There are two main reasons for this—the difficulty involved in making sense of the sentence 'the organization is trying to achieve something' and the complexity of most organization's aims and goals. To take the former case: as we have seen the sentence 'organization X is trying to achieve Y' can be quite meaningful. 'The University of London is trying to educate students'; 'Imperial Chemical Industries is trying to make a profit'; 'Glasgow Royal Infirmary is trying to cure patients'—would all be instantly understandable to most people. Attempts to translate these sentences into other sentences about what Professor A or Manager B or Doctor C is trying to do would be misleading. These sentences have a logic of their own.

The second difficulty, however, about the complexity of most organizations' goals, is much more important. In the first place, it is not very informative to be told that the university is trying to educate students, or a firm is trying to make a profit, or a hospital is trying to cure patients. They are unexceptionable phrases—in fact, 'trying to educate students', 'trying to make profits', 'trying to cure patients' are almost locked into the meaning of a university, business firm and hospital. One might, in fact say that they are not so much the goals of these organizations as their necessary conditions, in the sense that these organizations do not exist in the absence of these goals. Secondly, once one goes below these almost trivial statements of the goals of the organizations, and starts to dig into the hard empirical ground of what particular organizations have what particular goals, then a virtual Pandora's Box is uncovered. For it is quite meaningful to claim that the University of London is trying to help the British economy, that it is trying to become more efficient, that it is intent on establishing itself as the leading educational institution in the history of political thought, that it is concerned with improving its postgraduate research work and that it has as a goal the support of the city's cultural organizations by allowing itself to be represented on them. All of these could reasonably be claimed as goals of the University of London. Moreover, they are not contradictory or—in these examples—even competing goals. The problem then is to create a useful way of categorizing such goals. This would allow us to begin to draw up a profile of the priority placed upon certain types of activity by the organization, to assess rationally their value to the organization, to start to understand why certain activities are authorized and so on. Thirdly, this complexity often *does* mask contradictory or competing goals. A supermarket may install a security system of internal television cameras, various other electronic warning devices and patrolling security personnel, which may cost more to maintain than the value of goods stolen. A university may wish to graduate first-class students, but have an appointments system which guarantees the recruitment of mediocre faculty members. A business firm may be maintaining its image of public benefactor to the community at the expense of its profits and perhaps its ultimate survival.

The complexity of goal analyses is compounded by the fact that we have to examine the behaviour of particular people in particular organizations to discover what the goals of the organization actually are. It is, however, quite a different matter to describe the goals of the members of the organizations, whether as individuals or as groups, as the goals of the organizations. Assuming, however, that we discovered an organization whose goals were absolutely identical with the goals of one person or one group or all the people in the organization, then that would not oblige us to stop talking about the goals of the organization. Louis XIV may have needed the state to reinforce his egotism. Stalin had frequently to authorize his own aims in the name of the Soviet Communist Party. Nevertheless, keeping that last distinction in mind, it is true that we often have to scrutinize people's behaviour as well as organizational documents to discover what exactly are the goals of the organization. This is because we cannot take at face value the various formal documents there are in existence—not only because, as we have suggested, they may be too general or may mask a whole number of other activities, but also because of the fact that often there is a discrepancy between the so-called formal or stated goals of an organization and the actual or real or operative goals that people are pursuing in the name of the organization.

In order to illustrate some of the difficulties incurred in the use of the notion of an organization's goals, it may be helpful to take an example of one organization, in this case the creation and beginnings of the Scottish Business School. At the formal level, one might think that there would be no opposition to the statement that the aim of such a school, like the other Business Schools in this country, is to educate potential managers in the skills and techniques of management. Just as we produce doctors from Medical Schools, so we might just as easily (at least in principle) produce managers from Business Schools. However, even at this first stage, there are powerful arguments against such a stated goal. In the first place, some philosophers of education would suggest that there is something (almost) contradictory in the very idea of *management* education, that, as education is concerned with the 'whole man', to segment out a proportion as *management* education is to misunderstand seriously the nature of education. Again, it has been pointed out that whereas in Medical School there are agreed subjects for study—physiology, anatomy, pharmacology, for example—and accepted bodies of knowledge within these agreed subjects, in Business Schools there are no such agreements and no such accepted bodies of knowledge. The old Platonic argument that just as we leave gardening to the profession of gardeners so we should leave governing to the profession of politicians has all the same strengths and weaknesses when applied to the idea of leaving managing to the profession of management.

Moreover, most critics have asserted that placing Business Schools within universities tarnishes the image of neutrality that universities ought to possess in order to pursue successfully teaching and research. Business Schools, they maintain, are predominantly concerned with employers' problems—improving financial controls, marketing, labour turnover, productivity and the like—and tend to be involved in these problems on the employers' terms. By consciously allocating resources to the training of managers, it is argued that the university is taking sides in industry and thus bolstering up a system of economic and industrial relations which, at worst, it should be neutral about, at best, it should be actively opposing. Allied to this criticism is the claim that Business Schools are based on a harmony theory of industry, which again flies in the face of reality. For example, to managers, workers' wages are a cost: to workers, wages are their main, usually sole, source of income. Managers must keep costs down and workers must drive incomes up. And that's all there is to it—a permanent conflict of interests reinforced by the authority system of our society. To sum this point up: here we have an example of an organization where the formal goal—of educating students or potential managers in management—may be seriously discussed as being competitive with other former goals of the university, the advancement and dissemination of knowledge in all its branches.

The argument for the creation of Business Schools was won in the early sixties in the United Kingdom. In February 1970 a Scottish Business School was founded and an Academic Executive Committee, composed of senior academics from the Universities of Edinburgh, Glasgow and Strathclyde, was formed to co-ordinate existing facilities in the three universities and to define the requirements for future development. At the same time, it was announced that the Council of Industry for Management Education intended to divide £2 million equally between Scotland and the Midlands/Yorkshire region for Business School development. As the universities mainly concerned with management education in Scotland, these three agreed that the University of Strathclyde should be given £200,000 from the allocation, in order to help create the residential facilities required for special work in post-experience courses, with the remainder equally divided between the three universities. In January 1971 they announced that the Scottish Business School's inaugural programme of courses would begin in October 1971— as the press release of the time stated 'only by the closest co-operation between the universities who will house the three divisions of the School could the arrangements have been made with such expedition and made, in fact, in advance of our receipt of the funds we have been promised'. Again, one might reasonably maintain that an early goal of the Scottish Business School was and is to be in receipt of these substantial sums of money. It was also claimed at the same time that the Scottish Business School had made a good start towards creating the right conditions to develop rapidly as a major centre for management education and research, capable of providing substantial benefits for British and Scottish industry and commerce.

The goals of the Scottish Business School include not only the obvious ones of teaching management to students and researching management subjects within organizations, but also the nationalist one of furthering Scottish interests within the United Kingdom complex of Business Schools and universities with a sizable intellectual stake in the management of the economy. But, of course, the Scottish Business School had other goals to fulfil. There was a series of goals concerned with finding out what courses, type of course, size of course, and the like should be offered, that would provide these substantial benefits for the Scottish economy. Structures had to be created to facilitate the fulfilment. Ways had to be devised of informing people of its existence. An emblem for the School had to be designed, premises for its administration had to be found, brochures advertising its wares had to be written up, printed and distributed, and distribution points had to be found. Other goals were concerned with recruitment of staff to teach the courses being offered and to administer the School. A policy had to be worked out to ensure equal representation of the three universities in the activities of the Scottish Business School and also to ensure representation of the teaching members, who were to be mainly **drawn from the three universities, in the committees of the Scottish Business School. In other words, goals of education, environment, recruitment and representation** were among the main aims of the agents of the Scottish Business School.

The Scottish Business School is a fairly straightforward organization; at the time of writing (1973), it has one full-time secretary and typist, housed in three large rooms in Glasgow. It does, however, vividly draw attention to the complexity of organizational goal analysis. It does not help us to subsume most of these goals under one 'main' or 'real' goal, to assert that all these others are means to the end of educating students for management. The 'end' of management education is not something we can take for granted, as given, and which can be attained by various means. Often the 'means' we use affect or determine the ends. A system of financial control, for example, introduced to facilitate some other work, can itself become the main focal point of the organization. It is conceivable that the Scottish Business School could become in the future a monument to inertia, if the three universities concentrate on equitable relationships as their main aim, rather than, say, the improvement of the Scottish economy. Certainly, by the spring of 1973, that thought was common currency among some of their teaching members.

As one would expect, of course, in such a collaboration among organizations, many conflicting ideas have in fact been conceived, proposed and debated, since the very beginning of the Scottish Business School. It may even be comfortably held that this is the very stuff of organizations, a point we shall look at more closely in later chapters. But the fact that there are groups within the Scottish Business School—the teachers, the lay interests, the representatives of the three universities—who have their own, sometimes competing, goals and interests is, of course, an important consideration when one comes to make sense of particular activities and operations of the Scottish Business School. These goals and interests are not themselves the goals of the School. If one discovered, however, that an extraordinary amount of resources was legitimately flowing into the three universities without a resulting increase in the amount of teaching and research in management subjects, then one could reasonably posit that one of the real goals of the Scottish Business School was to act as a front organization for the aggrandizement of the individual university constituents.

It can easily be seen, then, that, with the simplest of organizations, the identification and analysis of goals may be quite difficult. We know, for example, of a small firm where the managing director is the son of the founder, the sales manager is the managing director's son-in-law, the works manager is the managing director's brother-in-law and the cashier is the managing director's sister. Presumably, when these appointments were made, the managing director had very much in mind his role as a member of his family, as well as that of chief executive of the small firm. It would, however, be wrong to assume automatically that here we have a case of the managing director pursuing organizational goals as managing director and personal goals as a relation of the sales and works managers and the cashier: what we *do* have is a small firm that has, in addition to its obvious goals of survival, profit, quality and the like, the extra goal of supporting the founder's family. But if we discover that the sales manager is in turn recruiting his friends into the firm by subterfuge, then here we can distinguish between the sales manager's organizational goal of improving the sales performance of the firm and his personal goal of looking after his friends. Often the boundaries between organizational and personal goals are blurred, but that does not mean that one cannot clear them up.

Is a useful classification of organizational goals possible? A definitive classification may be illusory because the goals of the individuals who will shape the goals of the organizations will be infinite. But one can suggest categories of goals that should be helpful in an introductory examination of the goals of any particular organization. The first set would distinguish formal or stated goals from real or operative ones; as we have indicated earlier, sometimes what an organization claims it is trying to achieve and what it is actually doing may be two different things. Another set would distinguish what the organization is producing from how the organization sets about fulfilling its productive role. Yet another set would distinguish internal goals about production and methods, from external, environmental goals of recruitment, standing, resources and the like.

Although, as we suggested, no satisfactory typology exists at the moment, categories of goals are not difficult to create. What we are concerned to demonstrate is that, in looking at an organization, one has to be aware of the range of activities in which an organization is involved. How one describes any particular goal may be best settled by finding out why one is interested in goal analysis in the first place. One of the outstanding characteristics of goal analysis is that it is frequently back-to-the-wall talk. When there are questions about the nature of the activities of the organization, when some knotty, apparently intangible organizational problem is at hand, then the question, 'what are we trying to do?' is usually raised. An interesting analogy may be with concern over natural rights, which tends to emerge when some profound injustice, like the Final Solution, has been perpetrated, and human beings, in desperation, have to argue for fundamental moral values.

People may be, and often are, confused or ignorant about what are the aims of their organizations. This is by no means always because of their personal deficiencies. Information about goals, as we have pointed out, is sometimes very difficult to obtain. However, if their roots are recognised, controversies of this sort are amenable to resolution through processes of clarification and information. What are not resolved by these processes are controversies about what ought to be the case—people may be in perfect agreement over what is the case concerning organizational goals, and at the same time be in total disagreement about whether this state of affairs is worthwhile. When organizational goals are called into question in this way, the organization may be faced with a problem concerning what is sometimes referred to as its 'legitimacy'. Many writers refer to the goals of an organization as things which serve to "legitimize the organization's existence" in the eyes of some group or another. This notion of legitimacy has no necessary connection with the circumstances of the creation of organizations. It has to do with issues concerning the rights and wrongs of organizational aims and their related activities.

First of all, people may have reservations about, or disagree with, the actual goals of the organization. Academic members of the university may strongly object to management education as one of the goals of their university. A chemical company which begins to produce napalm may have to cope with moral objections from some of its members. No doubt many civil servants in Germany in the early 1930s felt uneasy about the directions governmental activity began to take under the Nazi government. Secondly, organizations are normally committed to certain procedures for deciding on goals. People may disagree over the ways in which goals are decided upon, irrespective of what these actual goals turn out to be. Academics might not object to universities taking on the goal of management education, but become very upset if what they regard as proper procedures were not adhered to when the decision to undertake such a goal was made. Sometimes it is the case that when an organization makes a radical departure from its usual aims, although using its conventional and unquestioned procedures in arriving at the decision, for some people these procedures may be regarded as unsatisfactory. For instance, the British government's recent 'entry into Europe', using the customary parliamentary processes, was seen as such an extraordinary step for a government to take that many people felt that extraordinary democratic procedures, such as plebiscites, should have been used, in order to ensure the 'legitimacy' of the decision by the electorate.

A third distinction to be borne in mind when we consider situations in which organizational goals are in dispute involves the association of particular types of goals. An obvious example of this is the 'profit' goal of industrial firms in our society. People who may have little or no objection to the services and conditions actually provided by industry, nor objections to the generally autocratic internal procedures by which such goals are decided, may still be very upset over the fact that these are pursued with the intention of making a profit. An example of this which sometimes gives rise to a great deal of moral indignation is that of food-producing organizations purposely destroying large amounts of their products in order to maintain a high level of prices, at a time when millions of people are suffering from malnutrition.

In analysing controversies of this nature, care must be taken about the meaning of terms such as 'profit'. All organizations use things up, wear out machinery and so on, and must ensure that further supplies and replacements are forthcoming. 'Profits' may also refer to financial payments necessary in order to maintain an adequate capital supply by investors in the organization. It may further be used to refer to financial returns over and above that which is regarded, by some people at least, as adequate. All of these meanings must be separated out if we are to understand any particular controversy over 'profit' as an organizational goal.

It is also the case that disagreements over goals such as profit may occur because they are pursued in relation to particular sorts of production goals. Someone might be unperturbed by the idea of making plastic Christmas trees for a profit, but be upset, say, over the collection and distribution of medical supplies of blood at a profit.

Many examples of controversy about combinations of organizational goals may, of course, be found in non-profit organizations. In a hospital, disagreements can arise about the relationship between the main goal of curing illnesses and the goal of ensuring adequate training and research conditions. How they are resolved may have important consequences for the position of the hospital patient and raise questions about the role of a patient as an object of use in training and research. In summary, then, people may question the 'rightness' of the output goals of an organization, the procedures by which organizational goals are determined, and the association of certain types of goals with each other.

We started this part of the discussion about organizational goals by raising the notion of 'legitimacy' and then proceeded to discuss possible situations in which disagreement might occur over what ought to be the case as far as organizational goals are concerned. The legitimacy of organizational goals is questioned when people disagree with them as expressions of what ought to be the case. This, though, is a 'weak' and non-specific way of using the concept of legitimacy. The same word is used to refer to a variety of things which, while sharing a very general characteristic, at the same time differ in important respects. Using a term in a weak way like this may then lead us to emphasize what might be a fairly unimportant, shared characteristic of these things, and to neglect or ignore altogether important differences among them.

For a start we should be careful to distinguish between 'legitimacy' and 'legality'. The question of the legitimacy of an organizational goal is distinct from the question of whether or not it contravenes a law of the land. Recognizing this distinction allows us to analyse many important issues concerning organizational goals. For instance, an organization may be legally constrained to maintain a particular organizational goal towards which its authorized agents have a great deal of antipathy. The British Overseas Aircraft Corporation is pressured by government to pursue a certain level of return on its capital investment. On occasion it has also been bound to provide flights to certain parts of the world which detracted rather than added to this financial goal. These flights could properly be described under the heading 'public service' or 'organizational prestige' goals; the point is that the organization was bound to provide them, and as such it might have regarded them as necessary evils. The notion of legitimacy is usefully used in connection with people's *moral* evaluation of such things as organizational goals. Laws may themselves be the subject of such evaluation. "Is it legal?" is not the same question as "Is it right?"

Secondly, we must be careful to distinguish between legitimacy, a response of positive assent to the moral rightness of something, and responses of conformity based on such things as habit, convention, self-interest, or the fatalistic belief that things just cannot be altered for the better, anyway. Conformity to, or lack of overt disagreement with, organizational goals should not be taken to mean that consensus exists over their legitimacy. Thirdly, we should note that not all questioning of organizational goals raises the issue of their legitimacy. Disagreement may take place over whether or not particular goals should exist, or over the priority rating given to those organizational goals acknowledged to exist, without this agreement being of a moral nature. These sorts of disagreements are best characterized as 'prudential', 'practical' or 'technical' disagreements. The managers of an organization may formally debate among themselves over, say, the quality standards or range-of-production goals, either because they disagree over the technical question of the relation between such standards or range of variety and the profit goal, or because they each place differing emphasis on the importance of different goals, some perhaps wanting to pursue profit at the expense of reputation, others quality at the expense of market and so on. These disagreements may take place without the legitimacy of any particular goal being questioned.

Finally, the question "legitimate to whom?" should be asked. We referred earlier to the fact that many writers talk of organizational goals as the means by which existence of the organization is legitimized in the eyes of society. The metaphorical reference to society's eyes should not bar us from wanting to know more precisely whose opinions on legitimacy are being referred to. Also, while many people, groups, or organizations may articulate opinions about the legitimacy of an organization's goals, a crunch question will concern the strengths of these opinions. To what extent can an organization afford to ignore certain people's opinions?

Our discussion of the possible sorts of controversies which may occur over organizational goals rests on at least two important assumptions. First of all, we have rightly assumed that goals are not unchanging, fixed points in the world of organizations. Secondly, a related assumption we have made is that organizational goals are subject to changes that result from human deliberation and choice. Controversy over goals which stems from people seeking to change 'what is' to 'what ought to be' rests on the belief that changes can occur if men so decide.

Perhaps the clearest instance of the need for an organization to abandon one of its goals is when it has been achieved. A political party while out of office may have as its main goal the acquisition of power, yet on its being victorious at the polls or by means of a revolution, this particular goal would drop out, perhaps to be replaced by the goal of ensuring that it stays in power. A society aiming at collecting funds for the support of research into cancer would have to change its aim if cures for cancer became easily available at chemist shops. A hospital, intent over a period of years on planning and administering the building of an intensive care unit, will have to drop that goal once the unit is established. As organizations achieve their different kinds of goals, then these goals are usually dropped and different ones put in their place. The Chinese Communist Party is rare in its desire to retain its revolutionary impetus after it has become the effective ruler of China; most other Communist parties have rejected their revolutionary aims once they have acquired political power.

Of course, there are many other reasons why an organization should change its goals. The invention of new products can force the old ones off the market; the organizations that made valve radios have changed to transistorized ones or to some other product. Or again: the introduction into the market of a competitor who sells a similar commodity, but at a higher quality or lower price, may force an organization to alter its own goal about its commodity and the market. Similarly, if another organization enters the market with a different product which becomes a competitor, then the organization will usually have to change its goals. The marketing of cassettes in the sixties is a most visible (and audible) example. Ideological reasons will sometimes play a part in goal determination—in the weak sense of the prevailing fashion of the time, or in the stronger sense of changing aesthetic and moral beliefs. Organizations that traded in slaves may have resented the increasing public enlightenment over the question of slavery, but they still altered their goals of buying or selling slaves.

A final point we would like to make about goals relates to the managerial interest in organizations. Interest in what an organization is trying to achieve increased in the sixties throughout the country, with the introduction into many industrial companies of a management technique called 'management-by-objectives'. With this technique, organizations were asked to identify their goals in measurable terms of money, time, resources and so on. Those objectives were in turn broken down throughout the system, so that particular managers and officers of the organization would be able to see clearly what they were supposed to be aiming for over a set period. One of its most recommended ways of introduction into an organization was for the superior and subordinate to spend a considerable amount of time obtaining agreement on the subordinate's targets for, say, the next twelve months. The superior would then in turn clarify his objectives with his superior. In this way, managers would be better able to identify problems within the organization and would also be able to monitor their own, or their subordinate's performance. Goal talk became very fashionable, and by the late sixties had spilled over into other areas of activity, like the Civil Service and the hospital services.

Management-by-objectives has been aptly described as a 'do-it-yourself hangman's kit', for in agreeing to targets and objectives as attainable within some identifiable period, the manager is consciously committing himself to their attainment. It is putting your head on the chopping block. Many managers in fact regard it as a device by their superiors for watching and controlling their work more closely, and it is not unknown for managers to set up informal restrictive practices to beat the system. There are other difficulties, too—the system may be interpreted as being imposed, and personal commitment by managers consequently more difficult to obtain, or the inevitable increase in paperwork and appraisal meetings may generate resistance and possibly cynicism, resulting again in a drop in motivation—but perhaps the major flaw in all the management-by-objectives schemes of the sixties was their limited view of the goals of the organization. At best, various production goals might have been accurately pinpointed; at worst, the management might not have focused on any of the goals of the organization.

CHAPTER 4

The Importance of Structure

Often the only meaning that the word organization has for people is structure. When they think of an organization they often think of two-dimensional charts, with the head of the organization at the top and various boxes labelled with job titles or names placed below the box at the top, usually joined by uninterrupted lines or with arrows to indicate the communication or authority systems inside the organization. Reorganizing, in fact, often means restructuring, changing the boxes around.

Some ordering of activities is necessary if an organization's objectives are to be achieved. If you, as the producer-manager of a recording company, want to make a record of a group of young musicians which you think will be popular, then you will probably find yourself involved in the following activities. You will start discussions with the group of musicians and the musical director or arranger, who may be a member of your recording company. As a result of these discussions, the musical director may ask the personnel department to find him some extra musicians for the studio recording, in addition to the usually nameless session men who frequently accompany young pop stars. You yourself may now be in consultation with the recording engineer, who will be responsible for the technical equipment and the quality of the recording. After the actual recording, you will be involved with the recording engineer, improving the tapes. The best tapes having been selected, they are then sent to a department which concerns itself with transforming them into records. This in itself is a complicated manufacturing process which involves various operations. Once a proper record (the stamper, as it is called) is made, then the process is ready for mass production. During this period, other activities have also taken place. Some people in the recording company will have been costing the total operation—the amount of overheads that this particular record will have used up—while others will be concerned with the promotion of the record through discotheques, review journals and straight advertising. Others still are concerned with ensuring that copies of the record are available in the six thousand-odd possible outlets for records that exist in the United Kingdom. These—and many other activities—will result from your desire to make a popular record. Moreover, a number of these activities will be similar and will be grouped into various departments within the record company—manufacturing, recording, accounting, marketing, selling, and personnel. In each of the departments, there will be employees who are skilled in the operation of these activities.

It is along such lines that organizations are structured. An acceptable, if commonplace, definition of organization structure would be 'the established pattern of relationships among the components or parts of the organization'. Even if your record company had no organization chart, one could soon be drawn up. We could find out what all the people in the offices were supposed to be doing, who they were responsible to and for, their job titles and so on, and soon we would be able to sketch out the anatomy of the organization in an organization chart.

Such charts have their uses. They are useful introductions into the structures of organizations, for they are able to suggest the size of the organization as well as its major activities and the degree of hierarchical levels. Many organizations have such charts with varying degrees of sophistication and will produce them readily on demand. But they have limitations. In the first place, they do not usually indicate the scale of the power of each box. Does the occupant of each box carry the right to fire the members of the boxes below him? Sometimes yes, sometimes no. Secondly, they cannot indicate how the people represented by the boxes relate to one another. Nor, of course, can it tell us how the organization is perceived by its members, far less inform us of how the organization will work in practice.

When we speak of the structure of the organization, however, a great deal more than organization charts is intended. We have to find out the habits of the organization, its rules and procedures, its policies and regular arrangements, before we can put forward the organization's complete anatomy. At this point the study becomes more complicated. We have to find out how the organization's rules and procedures operate in practice, compared to how people in the organization assume they work. None of this is easy. The simplest task is to find out the prescriptions about how the organization's members should be behaving, for this will probably be recorded in various organizational manuals, agreements, documents, policy statements. A number of manufacturing organizations, for example, forbid employees to leave the office during working hours without written permission, or to take part in any meetings of employees during working hours without permission. Often, however, such prescriptions are poorly communicated, or so downright offensive that alternative procedures are built up. The same conflict arises in many other kinds of work systems. One can eventually recognize the discrepancy between what is being prescribed and what is actually happening. Nor is that the end of the matter, for we can still ask: are these prescriptions the right ones? And is what is happening something that ought to happen?

We can see, then, that to describe more fully the structure of an organization takes us into many areas of inquiry. We have to find out what are the prescribed activities of members and the rules and obligations that define positions. We also need to know how members interpret these prescriptions and how procedures work out in practice. To achieve this, we have to read documents, talk to people and observe behaviour. Assuming, however, that we can identify these areas and can give a full account of an organization's structure, we are still left with a number of important questions. Why is the organization structure as it is? Can it be changed easily? What are its determinants? Are some structures more suitable for some tasks and less suitable for others? Are some structures better than others?

A measure of how importantly an organization values its structure can be seen in the University of Birmingham's appointment in January 1971 of a review body to "consider the role, constitution and functioning of the University of Birmingham and to make recommendations to Council for any desirable changes". The committee, it is reported, met over the next twenty months for 51 days, heard 38 witnesses, read 81 documents submitted for the first draft of its report and finally, in November 1972, recommended a number of changes, including a number of comments on the structure and functioning of departments, faculties, court, council and senate. Questions on participation and procedures for appointment were also examined. That the recommendations may not be wholly accepted by the university does not in any way detract from the importance of the committee's work, or from the significance that the university gave to it in the first place.

The dominant type of organizational structure in our society is bureaucratic. Bureaucracy is a style of organization which has penetrated most social institutions of industrial societies. In a bureaucracy, the work of the organization is broken down into areas of competence and responsibility, and the people appointed into such work are regarded in the light of the technical and professional skills they can bring to bear. The organization is structured hierarchically, with the higher offices supervising the lower ones, authority carefully defined, compensation graded in accordance with responsibility, promotions and career advancement on the basis of seniority and achievement and with an appeals system built into the machinery of government. The whole organization will run on guide lines or general rules, which will ensure that the exercise of arbitrary power, favouritism and the like, cannot be openly pursued. The British Civil Service might be seen to approximate to the main characteristics of this form of organization. No connotations of 'red tape' or inefficiency are implied in this usage of the notion.

This form of organization has become so firmly entrenched in our thinking that it is difficult to imagine any alternative principles upon which we could construct organizations. Yet, despite the clear-cut strengths of the bureaucratic form, a great deal of critical attention has been paid to it. Critics, usually through field studies of actual organizations, have discovered that bureaucratic practice sometimes falls short of its promise, or that it is accompanied by unintended and disadvantageous consequences. However, few have written off bureaucracy altogether. Rather, critics have suggested ways in which its weaknesses may be remedied. These suggested changes have been limited and reformist, rather than revolutionary in nature. They are variations on what remains a basically bureaucratic theme. It is important to note, however, that the type of criticism of the bureaucratic model varies with what particularly upsets the critic about bureaucratic organization. There are a number of different critical approaches to the study of bureaucratic structure. First of all, a general problem which has concerned students of bureaucratic structures is that of power, the conditions in which it is exercised and certain beliefs that may grow about these. The bureaucratically structured organization is built on a set of principles at odds with democratic decision-making and popular control. In a bureaucracy, it is argued, goals appear as given, and fixed. The organization comes to be regarded as a technical machine-like instrument for the achievement of externally decided-upon ends. Policy aims are fed into the bureaucratic organization from the top, the object being to have these aims implemented through a series of more and more detailed directives, down through the closed set of boxes that constitute the bureaucratic structure.

This general concern about bureaucratic power has a number of aspects. First of all, the view of the bureaucratic machine as a neutral technical instrument of goal implementation is grossly misleading. If questions are raised, for example, about the nature of the goals, or how they are set, then these are often directed to places *outwith* the bureaucratic organization. In government, for instance, policy formulation has been conventionally regarded as something upon which government ministers engage. Civil Servants implement policy, although, of course, it is acknowledged that they have an important, advisory relationship with the policy makers. Democratic control over the Civil Service is assumed to be ensured through Ministers responsible to Parliament. The bureaucrats are servants of these Ministers. If such a dichotomy between ends and means, between goal formulation and goal implementation, is taken for granted, then the hierarchical authority structure of the bureaucratic organization seems right. If, as we suggested in Chapter Three, this dichotomy has little relation to reality, then the bureaucratic structure becomes problematical. For a start, the relationship between Minister and Civil Servant can no longer be regarded as merely technical, and therefore properly hidden from view. This relationship becomes critical and if democratic determination and control of organizational goals are to be assumed, it must be brought out into the open and subjected to scrutiny. This appears to be an increasingly recognized viewpoint, yet the last major organizational investigation of the Civil Service (the Fulton Committee of 1966/68) had explicitly excluded from its remit the study of Minister-

Civil Servant relationships. The Civil Service is often referred to in the Committee's Report as a machine or mechanism. Consequently, any structural problems were identified and defined as technical defects in a machine system, to be repaired, replaced, oiled or redesigned. Indeed, to the extent that the recommendations of the Report have been carried out, the notion of the Civil Service bureaucracy as a neutral machine controlled by machine-minders has been reinforced. The Fulton Report may be seen as a triumph for closed politics, a defeat for those who wish to strengthen democratic government by-opening up the policy-making process.

The second aspect follows closely from the first. If all important policy decisions are believed to be determined outwith the main organizational structure, then the principles on which such a structure should be built will be strictly bureaucratic. The bureaucratic structure is efficient for transmitting information downwards. However, if achieving goals is seen not merely as a mechanistic problem of means, of just telling people what to do, but one which may continually raise problems about goals, then the upward transmission of information about these goals becomes as critical as the downward transmission of orders. Bureaucratic structures are not so obviously suited to collecting information upwards. In fact, they operate most comfortably if the goals are seen as unchanging, once and for all problems requiring routine, recurring solutions. Because of this, the structure itself may systematically exclude the possibility of reappraising the problem in the light of changes. This problem is often referred to as one of 'bureaucratic resistance to change'. It is a problem which is accentuated by the fact that organizational structures, built on bureaucratic lines, help to build up expertise, rules, regulations, case histories and precedents, all of which become commitments to a particular definition of goals. If these definitions are challenged, the organizational structure may then become intransigent, with vested interests opposing redefinition of these goals. The problem of 'goal displacement' occurs, the means apparently becoming more important than the ends. It comes as no surprise to students of government to note that few, if any, radical redefinitions of goals have arisen from within the Minister-Civil Service department structure, where one would expect that the expertise and information for such changes would exist. Instead, occasional reports from specially set up commissions or private reformist organizations fill the gap left through Civil Service-Government default. It then, of course, becomes too easy for them to be ignored.

Another example is the way in which the structure of British universities has yet to accommodate to changes in the way students are interpreting their roles. The typical university structure assumes a more or less passive, one-to-one relation between student and teacher. The emergence of politically-motivated group activity took the universities by surprise in the sixties and exposed the inadequacy of their administration. In other words, the structure carries on servicing a goal which may have been rendered obsolete.

Thirdly—and again linked to the idea of bureaucratic structures servicing fixed goals—comes perhaps the greatest fear, the control of our lives by experts. Bureaucracy, it is believed, expresses the triumph of rationality in organized form. Underpinning this belief is the idea that advances made in science and technology have led to—or soon will lead to—the transformation of political activity in our society. Before the so-called technological revolution, politics was a messy business, mediating the conflicting goals of interest groups through creaking and inefficient democratic policy-making processes. Now 'truly rational, scientific' ways of proceeding have rendered these democratic procedures obsolete. With these new ways, it is said, we may properly identify our 'real problems' and produce the technology to solve them. Another variation on this theme is the belief that, whether scientifically or not, we all know and agree upon what *the* problems are—for example, increasing the gross national product—and all that is required is to set up the bureaucratic machinery manned by administrators and experts in order that they may be solved. It is not difficult to recognize in this a dominant characteristic of modern British politics, managerialism. Ironically, but hardly surprisingly, managerialism has failed to deliver the goods. The present Leader of the Opposition has recognised this and has now, at the time of writing, begun to build an electoral platform based on democratic grass-roots participation. For the first time in modern British politics, one of the two major political parties has begun an anti-organization campaign.

There are dangers, then, that we shall be led into believing that important social problems can be identified and solved managerially by expert officials and official experts. To admit otherwise and to reject the bureaucratic form would encourage the consideration of the main alternative form, of participation and democratic control. Of course, it could also be argued that bureaucratic structures tend to be run by groups of people to whose advantage it is to redescribe their own interests and problems as everybody's interests and problems. Managerialism is such a redescription.

A second group of criticisms is concerned with the demands bureaucratic structures make on members of the organization, and the consequences on their characters and personalities of meeting these demands. The structure of an organization may also be viewed as a required pattern of behaviour. At the very least, those who determine the formal structure have certain expectations as to how organizational members should behave and, usually, they have a considerable say in how people actually behave. These expectations have concerned many people, both critics and members of bureaucracies, primarily because they seek to shape relationships in such a way that people are treated as means rather than as ends in themselves. Bureaucratic relationships are seen as good to the extent that individuals subordinate their own particular prejudices, interests, values and ideals to those of the organization. In bureaucracies, it is argued, people may be treated impartially, according to the rules, and so on, but this equity of treatment is usually achieved at some cost to their humanity. In family, community and friendship relationships, persons are, of course, given to being 'useful' to each other, but these relationships do not usually consist of impersonal and calculative demands on one another as objects of utility. In bureaucractic organizations, it is pointed out, it is characteristically the case that there emerge certain ways of talking which directly reflect the required 'less-than-human' nature of the bureaucratic relationship. These include such phrases as, "Don't bring personalities into this"; "personally I don't like, it, but that's how it is"; "nothing personal, I'm just doing my job"; "orders are orders"; "ours is not to reason why . . ."; "this is our bible" (pointing to the organization rule-book); "we aren't a charitable organization, you know".

Perhaps more pointed than such language is the actual practice of work behaviour that is said to characterize bureaucratic jobs, particularly for those at the bottom of the organizational structure. Hour after hour, day after day, year after year, people as producers, and as employees, are expected and required to engage in routine, simple, repetitive, tasks. Adequate performance of this sort is all the organization may require; indeed, perhaps is all the organization can offer. While organizations may be said to live lives of their own, they rarely constitute complete worlds of their own, so naturally, organizational demands on people will, for the most part, be for impersonal and particularized effort. Moreover, the cost of the drudgery and boredom is justified on the grounds that obvious contributions to the common good result from the division of labour. Criticism of the bureaucratic structure, however, is not directed against the general fact of the division of labour; it is aimed at the extreme degree to which it may be carried in bureaucratic organizations. The man on the assembly line may be only an extreme and unrepresentative sample of all the members of bureaucracies, but it is the fact of his existence which raises serious moral questions about the increasing bureaucratization of organizations in our society.

The bureaucratic structure is built on a set of principles which constitute a rationale for the successful operation of the organization, but not on principles which derive from considerations of how people ought to be treated in a moral sense. Moreover, if acting in a creative, stimulating and self-disciplined way is not conducive to the operations of 'rational' organization, then many bureaucratic roles may require of their occupants a great deal less than they might otherwise have been prepared to give. Finally, in the bureaucratic structure, goal determination is not usually a matter of democratic vote by all organization members. Obviously, in an important sense, the fact that someone chooses employment in a particular organization, and so may choose *not* to be employed, will mean that individual has a moral responsibility for some of the actions of the organization. However, because the bureaucratic organization generally treats involvement in policy formulation as outwith the responsibility or *right* of most of its members, the tendency is to encourage a general belief that organizational goals can and should be treated with indifference—"orders are orders". In this way the relationship of the individual to the organization becomes conducive to the nourishing of a climate of moral indifference. This, then, may complete the picture of not just moral disquiet at the qualities of the demands made on persons by the bureaucratic structure, but, equally, of disquiet at the way people may be changed through the experience of conforming to these demands. Officiousness, authoritarianism, dependency, narrow-mindedness and moral indifference, are seen as the hallmarks of the bureaucrat—the type of person who, because of what he has become, cannot act in any other way, or worse, actually begins to enjoy acting as a cog in some larger machine.

Lastly, there has been a great deal of criticism of bureaucratic structure from those concerned with the managerial effectiveness of organizations. Case studies have revealed that, under certain conditions, highly structured work roles, rigid hierarchical relationships and a proliferation of formal rules prescribing work behaviour may act to lower the level of effective operation of the organization. Communication between people is affected, work effort is geared to the minimal levels laid down by the rules and the rules themselves may distort the direction of effort. Perhaps the major attack on bureaucratic structures has come from those concerned with the relationship between the organization and its environment. The management of an organization may so commit themselves to the maintenance of stable, predictable internal states of organizational affairs that the organization fails to cope with the degree of complexity and impetus to change that exists in its environment. Changes in markets and in technology may be so rapid that the traditional bureaucratic structure cannot easily adjust.

There are many determinants of an organization structure. First of all, there can be the clearly identified and ever-changing factor of fashion. Every decade brings its own popular managerial function or activity which bears upon the shaping of the organization. Computer departments and operational research units were among the fashionable innovative activities of the sixties; management-by-objectives, value and ratio analyses were the equivalent techniques. These activities and techniques are not simply additions to a structure which remains unchanging, but they in turn help to shape the structure. The introduction of a computer department may wipe out a whole layer of clerks whose work it replaced; it may, of course, generate a need for another layer of employees to cope with its many print-outs. The fashionable element in managerial decision-making, largely overlooked in studies of organization, is contained within the over-riding factor of ideology. By ideology we mean here the kind of beliefs that managers have about the world, about the nature of man and about the way society should be organized. Until recently, the language of organization and organization structure which the prevailing ideology endorsed was dominated by the language of elevation. Getting to the *top,* room at the *top, up* the organization, *top* people read *The Times, high* officials, lording it *over* an organization, or being at the *bottom* of the heap on the shop *floor,* pushed *down*—these, and many others, are ordinary phrases which lock our perspectives in certain ways. There would seem to be no obvious reason why we could not draw the traditional family tree or organizational chart upside down with, say, the managing director, Vice Chancellor, or Party leader at the bottom and still retaining the same communication lines or even authority system, but it would, to most people, be a shock. 'Power is at the top', as the saying goes, and reality adjusts to the language.

Yet, ideology and its peripheral element, fashion, although innovative and shaping reality, are themselves shaped by other factors, notably science and technology. The demand that scientific invention has made, through technology, on the shaping of our organizations is almost self-evident. The machine-age has virtually eliminated the craftsman who planned, programmed, worked and evaluated large elements of his work. Now, not only have the basic productive functions of manufacturing been broken down into simpler and simpler units (so that, in many cases even a modicum of intelligence becomes a positive handicap), but most organizations have become an increasing conjunction of specialists. Financial analysts, budget controllers, cost accountants, statisticians, production engineers and controllers, market researchers, public relations experts—organizations are cluttered up with such specialists. But technology does more than simply imply what kinds of specialists an organization must take on to fulfil its main goal—a nuclear power station would employ physicists, a newspaper would employ printers—it also influences the shape of the structure in less general ways. Where the organization is concerned with producing a standardized mass product—biscuits, shirts, motor cars, record players—then it would seem that an organization built for stable relations would be most appropriate. Mass production pays best on long runs, and with such long runs prediction of events is made easier, activities can become stabilized and routinized and the organizational structure is likely to be stable and relatively unchanging. But where the organization is concerned with manufacturing a few products at a time, say a space rocket or a boiler for an atomic plant, then prediction of events may be very difficult, new skills may have to be trained or recruited, the activities may be mainly innovative and hence the organization structure may be less stable and more changing. There is also some evidence to suggest that stable organizations attract people into their membership who prefer predictable, routine activities, and conversely, unstable organizations pull in members less concerned about security and conformity and more concerned about developing their own skills and professional careers.

Technology is a powerful influence, but there are still other determinants. There was no technological reason why the Soviet Ministry of Internal Security in the early fifties should have been responsible for border control, atomic energy, intelligence services, secret police activity, and prison camps, but the fact that it was so meant that the organization of these various activities would be complicated and diffuse. With such a large organization, certain characteristics inevitably emerge. Controls are difficult to operate, information is difficult to process, inefficiency is rife and competing power points appear in the system. The story has been told of a Soviet citizen taking a rifle into Red Square and firing a number of shots at Mikoyan's car. Red Square at that time was saturated with security guards, but they did not dare to act immediately without orders, because they could not be sure that the attempted assassination was not sanctioned by an even higher authority than Mikoyan. The guards were effectively paralysed until higher 'clearance' was obtained to shoot the offender. Political complexity, size and centralisation, all combine to paralyse the organization just at the point where the need for swift action is greatest.

The Soviet Ministry of Internal Security is not unique. The American Department of Defence is the largest organization in the world, employing millions of military and civilian personnel. Contained within it are the three main functional units based on land, sea and air warfare techniques, the intelligence services and the thousands and thousands of servicing units. On the face of it, it is unmanageable, and occasionally a story leaks out from the Department to reinforce this suspicion. In the early sixties, for example, it was discovered that various military departments had been establishing their requirements independently of one another. The Army was planning for a long war of attrition against the Russians and was intent on stocking up for a sizable conventional war that would take months, and perhaps years, to resolve. The Air Force, on the other hand, was planning on nuclear bombardment and was measuring its requirements in terms of hours, at the most a few days. Whatever else these policies demonstrate, they undoubtedly indicate a lack of managerial control at the top.

Although it is a comfort to know that large organizations are unmanageable—it is, after all, the sole saving grace of totalitarianism—the general tendency in our industrial societies is for organizations to grow in size. There are, of course, many criteria of size—revenue from sales being the favourite—but if we use the more obvious criterion of manpower employment, then already the number of British companies employing over 100,000 men and women—General Electric Company, for example, with over 200,000, British Leyland Motor Corporation and Imperial Chemical Industries with just under—suggests the existence of critical problems of structure. Moreover, the term 'multinational corporation' became part of our ordinary language in the late sixties. Certainly it is an increasing fact of life that companies whose homes are in one country, but which operate in other countries as well, have grown in the last ten years. It has been estimated that such companies will produce 50% of the world's goods by the year 2005, and 80% by the year 2040. One out of every nine workers in Scotland is employed by a U.S.-owned enterprise. It has been calculated that over half of Britain's car production and over two-fifths of its output of computers and refined petroleum products in the mid-sixties came from U.S.-owned companies. Patterns like these are established in other European countries, and are taking shape in the other continents. The organizations of multi-national corporations should provide a rich seam for budding organization theorists of the seventies. In the meantime, they draw attention to the importance of size in the shaping of the structure, although the factor of size will, of course, be influenced by the kind of technology with which the multi-national corporation is primarily concerned.

Because the organization can be shaped by so many factors—fashion, ideology, size, market, technology, environment—organization structures come in all shapes and sizes and generate their own peculiar sets of problems. The bureaucratic model has been, as it were, the benchmark for so many organizations that one could talk reasonably about all organizations being to a lesser or greater extent modifications of the bureaucratic model, but such talk is now much more questionable. There would appear to be three main reasons for this. First of all, technology as a factor in influencing organizations is now rampant in industrial societies, and this factor will be compounded by the industrialization of the Third World. As a prime example of contemporary technological innovation, the case of aerospace firms suggests that mechanistic structures should be buried, and that new structures will have to be introduced. The main focus of these organizations seems to lie in the area of co-operation and collaboration. The technologies involved are so complex that no one person or group of persons can be decisive in their utilization, and, as a result, a high premium has been placed on the ability of people inside the organizations to maintain and develop good working relations with their colleagues. Of all the spin-offs from the American aerospace programme, perhaps the most important is the managerial. One of us was recently told by an American executive of one such company, "we only fire people if they can't get on with other people". If this was the criterion of employment in British organizations, many of them, it has been suggested, would be devoid of personnel.

Another reason for seeking alternative models of organizations is the demand by organization members to have some say in the running of the organization. The origins of this demand are varied—in the nineteenth and twentieth centuries there have been many socialist and syndicalist groups that have proposed forms of 'workers' control' of business firms, while attempts to realize these ideas occurred in Russia in 1917, in Yugoslavia after the war, in Cuba after the overthrow of Batista, in China with the introduction of commune organizations, in Israel with the kibbutz. Judging the success of these and other organizations will, of course, take us straight back to the question of what are the goals of the organization. If they are to be judged on grounds of relatively uninterrupted and efficient production, then they may not be in the same league as their bureaucratic equivalents, but, if their main aims include that of member satisfaction and democratic control of the organization's activities, then, of course, they might be streets ahead. Whatever the case, structures are being consciously created at the moment which contrast with the previously dominant model of bureaucracy.

There is another reason for doubting the durability of bureaucratic forms of organization, and that is the psychology of the young generation. We are living in a time of great social change, when the traditional roles of being a grandfather and grandmother, father and mother, husband and wife, son and daughter, are all being overhauled and re-examined. People are living longer; separation, divorce and trial marriages are much more common, increasing numbers of mothers are employed in the economy—these and many other social changes are making us think more closely about the nature of our relationships with other members of our family and our friends and colleagues. One result of this rethinking has been the rise in commune and underground organizations among young people, notably in the United States. In these organizations, the way in which members relate to other members is considered seriously, and new concepts, or old concepts redefined, have been added to our language of organization structure—respect for others, responsibility, maturity, love, affection, kindness, sense of humour. Being introduced into our adult working lives are concepts previously reserved for our evening and weekend activities.

Organizational textbooks continually tell us that we are living in an organizational society. Certainly it is only in the last few years that organization as such has been singled out for special attention and become a respectable subject for study in university. But it is also a time when the word 'organization' has become closely tied up with the bureaucratic model of organization and some of the mud slung at bureaucracies has stuck on organizations. 'Organization-man' has been for some time a term of abuse. One paradox of our time is that, as we first prepare to study organizations systematically, we do so at a time when their predominant characteristics are under severe attack.

CHAPTER 5

People in Organizations

In Chapter One we said that an important reason for studying organizations was that they shape people's behaviour. They do this in two main ways. First of all, people are either forced, or paid, or in some way persuaded, to act as members of organizations. While organizations may lead lives of their own, they can only do so by intruding into the lives of human beings. The chapters on goals, structure and environment were, in a sense, demonstrative of this. Sometimes, however, using these concepts encourages us to neglect people's involvement in organizations, to the point where little or no indication is given that the subject-matter is *human* organizations. Secondly, by behaving as members of an organization, people, in a general way, may begin to act differently from the way they would have if they had not joined that particular organization. Characteristics leap to mind when we describe an individual as ex-Royal Air Force, an old lag or a public schoolboy.

The subject of organizational behaviour is a complex and varied field occupied by all the human and social sciences. If we were to extract from a university library all the volumes on the behaviour of people in organizations, then there would be gaps on many of the shelves of economics, sociology, anthropology, history and politics. Even if we were to collect only that literature which was entitled 'behaviour in organizations' or 'organizational behaviour', diversity of contents would be its most striking characteristic. This can be bewildering because one might expect those who study the same subject to agree on what are the most important problems and how they should be tackled. There are many reasons for the marked absence of unanimity between studies of behaviour in organizations. A major one is that such studies will depend upon the nature of our concern. The form this takes will lead us to select out of the wide and complex world of organizations only particular types, or aspects, of

E

behaviour. There are many ways of cutting a cake. The various forms of our concern will result in different principles of selection in the study of organizational behaviour. The aim of this chapter is to illustrate some of these principles of selection and their consequences.

First of all, we may be interested only in the behaviour of people in particular kinds of organizations. The events and activities selected for study may then owe more to the fact that they occur in that kind of organization than that they occur in organizations in general. For example, strikes, absenteeism, and labour turnover are phenomena more or less peculiar to organizations that employ people. They will not feature much, if at all, in studies of life in monasteries. The incidence, nature and causes of escapes will be an important subject for the student of prison life, but will hardly attract attention from those interested in university affairs. Participation in elections will feature in studies of behaviour in political parties, trade unions and perhaps churches, but rarely in business firms and schools. In each of these cases, a particular type of organizational context is implied or specified. Hence our surprise when we find them referred to in inappropriate contexts—strikes by monks, escapes by university students. It is interesting to note that students now occasionally have strikes, although these are for reasons different from those that occur in industry. In certain respects, universities are changing their nature and becoming more like industrial organizations. It has already been suggested that we should view the university as a factory—that, for example, the universities should be in charge of the students' grants and pay them out as wages and salaries. Fortunately, however, they have not yet become like factories.

Using a principle of selection based on one particular kind of organization will delimit the subject matter of organizational behaviour. Different organizations are vehicles for different activities—devotion and prayer in churches, collective bargaining in trade unions, study and learning in schools. Often, but on a relatively minor scale, similar behaviour occurs in different organizations. No doubt many students have uttered a prayer at examination time, and some people work for a living in trade unions. These, however, are incidental to the main types of activities that go in universities and trade unions. The operation of this principle of selection has led to the development of organizational analysis within many fields of study. The recent emergence of educational administration as a subject, for example, has been accompanied by an increase in the number of organizational analyses of the schools. Prior to this there were studies about teaching methods, classroom sizes and academic achievements, but hardly any accounts of how schools are managed or how the administrative structure of a school might affect the quality of teaching within it.

Perhaps the only major problem is that this kind of principle of selection may sometimes be used in a misleading way. Occasionally, a text on organizational behaviour will claim relevance to all organizations when, in fact, its contents are exclusively about business firms, or worse, about one particular kind of business firm. Or, someone might abstract a picture of organizational behaviour from a wealth of observations about, for instance, life in mental hospitals and then use this as a model to study other organizations. These other organizations might share a general characteristic with mental hospitals—for example, all their members may live on the premises. The activities of people in concentration camps, residential schools, merchant ships and monasteries are then grouped together, regardless of their obvious differences.

Secondly, we may be concerned with people's behaviour irrespective of the organization in which it occurs. Here the problem is that the principle of selection—*all* behaviour in organizations— is so general and diffuse that it becomes difficult to focus on any behaviour in a useful and informative way. An example of such a generalized approach is that which uses the organizing concept of role. With some students of organizations it has a central place. They define organizations as systems of roles and maintain that organizations will only function as a result of their members perceiving the nature of their roles and acting in such a way as to fulfil the requirements of their roles. The idea is not unattractive. Often we behave in organizations as we think others will expect us to behave. Young lecturers in a university often bore their students, who may be almost their contemporaries, by behaving in pretentious and over-academic ways—in other words, acting out how they perceive the job of a university teacher. Army sergeant-majors expect other people to see them as loud-voiced bullies with short tempers for mistakes. Recently a campaign by some air hostesses to alter the expectations that other people held of them centred on the issue of forcing the airline companies to employ less attractive girls. A role, then, is a relationship: a set of expectations connected with the performance of a particular task or tasks. From this central idea one can construct other interesting concepts. Role conflict, for example, could easily describe an organizational problem where an individual might experience unreasonable or incompatible demands from his superior or his colleagues. It might also describe a situation where the organization made demands on the individual which ran counter to demands made on him in other roles— for instance, as a trade unionist, or as a parent. Again, the ambiguity of a role can be experienced when an individual does not know what his superior or his colleagues expect of his performance, or the criteria they are using to judge his behaviour, or what the rights and responsibilities of his job should be.

One can obtain a lot of mileage out of such a notion, but it is not itself the key to understanding all behaviour in organizations. First of all, there lurks in the concept of role the idea of theatre— we are all actors, playing out our roles, to the different audiences of our colleagues, our bosses, our parents, our wives and our children. To act out a role suggests, however, that this is how we normally behave. We can only make sense of the claim that we are acting out a role if we can understand what it would be like not to act out a role. The notion of role is offensive, for it takes away from an individual his individuality and gives him a number of lines to speak. Secondly, the concept does not appear to give us room to interpret the same role in different ways. The young lecturer may relate much more easily to his students than his older colleagues, because he interprets the job of teaching quite differently. The air hostess may be a better air hostess because she puts more stress on the care and welfare aspects of the job rather than on glamour or sex-appeal. Nor does the concept indicate that the same role can be acted out in different ways in different organizations. The Clydeside foreman may have needed his bowler hat steel-lined to protect his head from 'accidental' hot rivets, but undoubtedly foremen in other industries safely went bare-headed.

Whether we use the notion of role or not, we might be

concerned with some *particular* aspects of behaviour in all organizations. For example, the extent to which technology is a factor in shaping the ways people behave has received a great deal of attention. So, too, has the quality and type of supervision. Also, the degree to which people's behaviour is characterized by some quality such as conflict, satisfaction, creativeness, or freedom from constraint, may provide us with a principle of selection with which to study people's behaviour in organizations. Or we might begin with a particular state of affairs within the organization, and investigate the extent to which behaviour contributes to it. How effective, for instance, are the activities of people from the point of view of organizational goals? Using such a principle of selection will involve detailing the various goals of the organization and then identifying behaviour which contributes towards goal achievement. An overall notion of organizational effectiveness may, however, be difficult to specify. Organizational goals, as we pointed out earlier, may conflict. The goal of rehabilitating convicts may best be served by managing activities and changing prison structures, which are out of line with the prison objective of preventing escapes. How effective is a prison which reforms a certain number of prisoners but lets another lot escape? Values and judgements about reforms and escapes will determine the answer.

Because any one of a number of such principles may be used, relating to the causes, experiences, characteristics and consequences of action, the contents of studies of organizational behaviour vary considerably. The same phenomena may be studied from different perspectives with different problems in mind. A study of behaviour in an industrial firm, which is concerned with describing and accounting for the distribution of material wealth in the organization and trying to arrive at an assessment of the economic viability of the organization, will be drawing on some of the characteristics and means of the same set of employees and shareholders of the organization as will a study which seeks to map out the justice or authority of the organizational structure. The people in the organization, their attributes, their behaviour in all its complexity, will not change as the study of them changes. The different perspectives will draw different pictures and be valuable for different purposes. Each, if it is to be useful, will have to square with the facts. As we have indicated, however, the idea is not to arrive at a neutral collection of information about organizational behaviour. Even if the study is aimed only to entertain, these facts will have to be organized, selected, and related to each other in amusing ways. Nobody falls about laughing over a neutral set of facts. This lack of consensus is not surprising. It might be worthwhile to ponder on the conditions of people in organizations that would need to obtain in order for consensus to become possible. One of the greatest degrees of consensus about behaviour that does occur is among students whose subject matter is laboratory-trained rats.

Much less straightforward are cases where organizational theorists disagree with each other over the way the same problem should be analysed. One fundamental problem, for example, is—why do men obey other men in organizations? Organizations are expressions of more or less planned strategies for the achievement of certain ends, and involve the collective actions of many people. How does behaviour contribute towards the requirements of these strategies? What reasons do individuals have for conforming to organizational purposes? How do they come to interpret their organizational situations as justifying their acting for such reasons? How do their organizational situations come to be arranged to produce these desired responses? These questions may be asked of behaviour in all organizations. The fact of obedience is perhaps the dominant fact of behaviour in organizations. Whether the student of organizations has a political, moral or managerial interest in organizational behaviour, the problem of obedience will, in one form or another, usually be prominent in his scheme of things. Yet on this problem a lack of agreement seems to prevail among theorists.

To the question, why do men obey, the study of behaviour in organizations will provide different answers. A person's reasons for joining a church and taking on the responsibilities of church membership will obviously tend to be very different from the reasons for gaining employment and becoming subject to the requirements of an industrial organization. And even if it could be shown that, in some respect at least, the same reasons might inform both—a desire for social prestige or wanting to meet the 'right sort of people'—the organizational situations which are arranged to produce desirable member behaviour will be very different. The disagreements that occur among theorists over the problem of organizational obedience are not, however, usually caused by the fact that they are each studying different sorts of organizations without being aware of it.

Assuming that this sort of mistake is not made, and that the problem is identified as trying to answer the question, why do people obey, then there are still disagreements over how the problem should be tackled and, consequently, different sorts of answers. The major problem for the person who wishes to tackle this will be how to identify and classify the different causes of individual conformity to organizational requirements. We may say of attending a church service, working at one's job, handing in an essay, that all are instances of behaviour which conform to organizational requirements. This common quality will be only the beginning of an analysis which seeks to understand the problem of obedience. The fact of an act being in conformity with the intentions, requirements, or expectations of someone or some group is important, but it is a rather limited sort of fact. We know from our experiences, and learn through our language, that there are many reasons why men come to obey. People may obey out of habit, or without thinking. They may do so willingly, because they want to, or because they feel they ought to, that it is right. They may act from fear, for themselves or for others, and from different sorts of fear—social disgrace, material deprivation, physical hurt. They may do so out of greed, or simply in order to earn a living. We are nowhere near exhausting the list of possibilities. To the extent that any one particular reason dominates a man's mind, then a satisfactory answer to the question, why did he obey, should contain that reason. But the theorist who asks this question is asking something different from the question, why does that particular person obey in that particular situation? He sets the question at a general level with the expectation, presumably, of arriving at a general sort of answer. This sort of answer will tend to ignore many of the kinds of distinctions that 'are evident in particular cases. The problem, then, is, why do we judge these lost distinctions to be unimportant?

To put it another way: the desire for economical and tidy generalisations may lead a theorist to herd together under the same label cases of obedient acts which, whilst they share the characteristics of being instances of obedience, nevertheless possess qualities which make them in important ways (not least for the persons obeying) very different types of events. What tends to happen is that, before investigating matters of fact about men's conformity to the intentions of others, the theorist makes a decision to interpret all actions which involve conformity as expressive of some dominant quality, so as to reduce all other distinctions that may be made about obedience to the status of sub-types of the dominant one. This might not be a very significant matter. The problem is that the theorist's choice of a dominant umbrella quality may be such as to make it very difficult to do justice to the great differences that do exist between different acts of obedience.

This problem is characterized by the mistaken use of the concept of power. If all the actions of men which are in conformity to the intentions of others are described as examples of power, being the quality of the relationships between men, then inhabiting this kettle will be the most odd collection of fish. 'Please close the door' and 'your money or your life' are both instances of ways in which it is possible to get others to do something that you want. To classify them both as illustrative of 'power attempts' and, if they are successful, as 'power relations', is to disregard the fact that they are different. The former is a commonplace reminder of polite behaviour, the latter is an extortionate act involving the threat of physical violence. To call both of them acts of power is not too helpful an exercise, because it classifies together two very disparate acts, and moves attention from the crucial difference between them. Part of this crucial difference, for example, is the distinction between willing and unwilling obedience. Analysing these distinctions as important sub-types of the genus 'power' means that we cannot then use the term to make what seem highly useful distinctions—for instance, to use 'power' as a quality of characteristically unwilling or coerced activity, and to use a word such as 'authority' to refer to acts which are in some sense willing.

Authority, like power, is another term that is often offered as the overriding, organizing concept for analysing problems in organizations. The sciences of human behaviour in organizations, mainly psychology, sociology and political science, all, at some time or another, invoke the concept as an explanatory device to account for, say, a local strike or a conflict between an administrator and a professional. Who has the authority to do what is, after all, an important organizational question. Why men obey other men is often settled by description of the authority of these other men. Understanding the nature of authority is often proposed as the key to understanding behaviour in organizations.

The trouble about this proposition is that it is not obviously true. In the first place, a number of observers have appeared to manage reasonable explanations without recourse to the subject of authority, which, at least, questions the claimed necessity of the concept. Secondly, and much more importantly, there is little or no agreement about the meaning of authority. Some writers have maintained that authority is simply legitimate power; others that it is rightly applied force; others again, that it is the right to expect performance from others; and still others who see it as the power to make decisions which guide the actions of other people. Now, of course, authority cannot be legitimate power *and* the power to make decisions which affect the actions of others, for some people have a power to make such decisions that we would unhesitatingly describe as illegitimate. A bank robber with a shotgun would have such a power in a bank, but it would be misleading to describe him as having authority in the bank. But even if we amalgamate these varying definitions, we are still left with two polarized views about authority. On the one hand, many social scientists have opted for the view that authority should be subsumed under the genus power; on the other hand, a few philosophers have denied this, maintaining that the main function of the concept of authority is to underline certain ways of regulating human behaviour in contrast to other ways, including ways indicated by the concept of power.

We may, however, distinguish different types of authority in organizations. The first type would be indicated when we speak about people being 'in' authority or appointed 'to' authority or being 'given' authority or doing things 'with' authority. The sense of these phrases is usually quite clear: they indicate a system of rules which determine who may legitimately do various kinds of action within an organization. It may reasonably be called organizational authority, but other writers have termed it rational authority. Regardless of the particular qualifying adjective, it is usually clear that all of these writers have in mind that having authority *means* being authorized, being empowered to do certain things. The fact that someone is licensed or elected or entitled by others to do something is usually another way of saying that he is authorized or empowered to do it. Serious conflict in organizations may occur when the system of rules determining the ways in which individuals come to be in authority are judged to be illegitimate by those under them.

A second type of authority relates to the amount of knowledge or skill that the person has in the organization. Training, competence, technical skill, past success, professional attitudes, ability, expertise, achievement, are locked into this type of authority: they provide the reason for the person's right to pronounce on certain organizational matters. An expert accountant or a good researcher or a clever navigator are commonplace examples of this type. But, of course, being 'in' authority and being 'an' authority are distinct. It is quite conceivable that someone who does not hold any position of authority is in fact an authority; it is often a source of criticism in organizations that people who have the first type do not in fact have any of the attributes of the second type. Incompetent teachers should expect harsh treatment from their students.

A third type rests on the personality of the actual individual. It is a fact of life that some people have a style of talking and relating to other people which is commanding, while others in the same environment may prefer to play a more passive role. This type of authority is harder to identify than the first two. A person who in one context may appear quiet or reserved could emerge as the powerful leader in another, as frequently happened in German concentration camps. But, whatever the difficulty in locating and identifying this type, it is usually easy to understand that some people, simply because of their personality, can be more authoritative than others. This is sometimes the popular meaning of charismatic authority.

Yet another type of authority rests in the realization by a person's colleagues that he is a morally good person. We mean here not only the appreciation by his colleagues that they trust and rely on him, but also that he is concerned with such things as improving the overall working conditions of his colleagues. It has been called the authority of integrity, of confidence, or, more straightforwardly, moral authority. It usually arises over a period of time when there has been a stable amount of interaction between members of the work group or organization. This type of authority, we shall be arguing later, is critical for the understanding of some problems in organizations. For example, one could easily imagine a schoolteacher or works manager or political leader who had acquired the first three types of authority. If, however, over a period of time, he has not established in others any confidence that he is concerned with more than his own self-interest, then he will not have any moral authority over his subordinates or with his colleagues. A great deal of niggling or backbiting or other forms of organizational strife usually indicate an absence of such authority.

A fourth way in which the study of behaviour in organizations may vary is due to the fact that any attempt to describe, explain, evaluate or change behaviour in organizations rests on some underlying ideas about the nature of man. These ideas will be of how 'man' basically is and why. Students may well agree on which particular organizational activities they want to study. They may agree also on the sorts of problems about that behaviour which ought to be resolved. Their work may nevertheless differ, because they do not share a common notion about the nature of man. This difference in their work will show in the key words they use to describe their human subject matter, in their selection and description of causes of behaviour, and in their means of arriving at reliable knowledge of these things. If they seek to change behaviour, the points at which they believe change ought to be attempted will also depend in part on the image or idea about man that they use. It will also tend to be the case that the ways in which they characterize the organizational situations of the people they are studying will rest in part on these ideas.

All these differences may emerge because they have each chosen and operated on different primary notions about human beings and their basic condition. The interesting and important thing to notice about this is that these differences are not erasable by an appeal to matters of fact. Factual considerations will play an important part in the way we come to assess the values of different models of man, but they will not be able to arbitrate between them. Indeed, it is the case that these models play a vital role in determining the shape of facts. How, then, do these models come about?

It is best to answer this question by, first of all, drawing on examples of these primary notions about human beings from our everyday language. There are commonly used linguistic devices through which these notions are introduced. Examples of these devices are phrases such as: "All men are inherently evil"; "essentially man is a being capable of perfection"; "when you get down to it all men are lazy"; "fundamentally, man is a rational creature". When it is particular classes or groups of people and not all mankind that is being referred to, these claims clearly serve a prejudicial purpose. "All Russians are devious"; "all Italians are cowardly"; "all students are irresponsible". When the reference group for the attribution of a quality is all men, and this attribute is assumed to be a built-in characteristic of what it is to be human, then the prejudicial nature of the move is disguised. Calling Italians cowardly, or Scotsmen mean, is to contrast these classes of people with, say, valiant Englishmen, and generous Americans. But if it is said that *all* men are inherently selfish, this can hardly function in the same way. Its logical status has the appearance of being equivalent to a factual statement, such as "all men are one-headed beings". Yet to call people selfish is to describe them from a moral point of view. It is to say that they are behaving in ways that are wrong. It is to assume that they should act differently—and that they can act differently. But if all men are said to be selfish, if this is regarded as a fixed, determinate part of their nature, then the assumption that they could behave differently, in an unselfish manner, is false. Now, there are many occasions on which we do refer to people's behaviour as unselfish. We can not only conceive of an unselfish act, we have all witnessed examples of it. How is this the case, if all men are selfish? The person who believes that all men are so, will have either to ignore blatantly the evidence that suggests that on occasion, at least, men have acted differently, or, more insidiously, he will redefine unselfish so that it becomes a sub-type of the class of acts which are selfish. So introduced into our language is the neologism 'enlightened self-interest', or the tortuous argument that, because men only act when they want to, even unselfish behaviour is really selfish.

What is the use of such images of man? At least two uses are discernible for the examples we have raised. First of all, to say that all men are selfish might be a belief that justifies an individual's refusal to behave unselfishly, a form of rationalization. Secondly, and much more importantly, it serves as a guide to action in relation to other people. These images help to regulate social behaviour. If all men are selfish, then their actions must be constrained by external means, in order for the common good to be served. (Unless, that is, you subscribe to the claim that the best way to serve the common good is by allowing all men to act selfishly.) If all men are naturally lazy, then in order to make them work you had better arrange to push them, watch them, promise them rewards and threaten them with punishment if they will not behave as you want. If you believe that basically all men are good, you will look for those things that may have caused them to act otherwise, and try to remove them, to allow men to act in good ways.

We are all caught up in this. Our behaviour is a function of our way of seeing human beings, and the point at which our behaviour becomes critical—when, for example, we are about to punish a child or make a worker redundant—is where we should stop to scrutinize the assumptions we are making about the nature of children or workers. Germans could live easily and sleep well at nights while the Jews were being systematically slaughtered, because Jews had been redefined out of the human race. Some Americans could remain unperturbed about the Vietnam war, because somehow Vietnamese people were not high on their list of important people. The authors know of one company where there is a high rate of dismissal by telephone on sites away from the head office, but not at the head office, where to fire a man would necessitate a face-to-face interview. One could hope that, if each of six million Germans had had to kill personally one Jew, there might have been millions of Jewish people who survived the war.

Are there many different ways of seeing human beings and on what does this seeing depend? Can they be changed and in what ways? We would suspect that there are an infinite number of ways of seeing human beings but that, as our perceptions are usually informed by our family upbringing, our education and our work environment, the chances are that, at any one time, there will be a few dominant ways of viewing human nature. In Europe, for example, the influence of Christianity has provided a language to describe human beings; concepts of guilt or original sin or charity or forgiveness or love come to us from centuries of discourse about the nature of man. In China, the ideas of Confucianism and Buddhism have shaped some of the political activities of the

Chinese Communist Party. Science, too, has increasingly offered language to describe man's nature and has now replaced religion, as the main source of new ideas about human beings.

What this comes down to is the following: one model proposes that there are a few born and trained to rule, some more capable of supervisory roles and a great many hewing wood and carrying water. The hierarchical structure of Plato's Republic would correspond to this view, with its philosopher-kings, guardians and workers. So would the British Civil Service, until recently, with its administrative, executive and clerical levels. The British Army has its officers, non-commissioned officers and other ranks (their spouses were similarly ranked as ladies, wives and women). At one time, the British Broadcasting Corporation had three services: a Third Programme for serious music and intellectual discussions, a Home Service with some serious music and a great deal of Grand Hotel music and a Light Programme with so-called popular music and comedy shows. Such a model provides a theory of motivation, a theory of organization structure, a theory of organization change and a theory of value. Once you have identified your station, you have come across your duties.

Until recently, in fact, such a model would have been synonymous with the idea of organization. As we pointed out earlier, when we were discussing the notion of organization structure, we often think of an organization in terms of one box at the top and increasing numbers of boxes spreading out from the top. It would be difficult to think of non-hierarchical ways in which one might build the Pyramids or dig for coal in the Rhondda Valley or lay a railway line across the United States. A few men of vision, some interpreters of that vision, and a great deal of sweated labour, could be said to be the only way in which such jobs could have been done. Sometimes, if such a view was challenged, the divine right of kings or some updated version of it was invoked to reinforce the system. There are still many organizations that are shaped along Platonic lines.

The last hundred years of scientific discovery and technological developments have eroded this Platonic model. The development of engineering suggested that a man should be viewed as a component in the total manufacturing process, of the same order as a lathe or boring machine. Just as machines need looking after, so do men. They need money to buy food and clothes and some protection from the weather. At the turn of the century came the first attempts to observe the behaviour of the worker on the shop floor and to recommend ways in which he may become more efficient. There is in the literature on organizations the now-classic story of the Pennsylvanian Dutchman who was guided by the American engineer Fredrick Taylor to increase his work performance from $12\frac{1}{2}$ tons of pig-iron a day to 47 tons. The idea which this story illustrates is that work could be analysed into its essential units, then recomposed into more effective and efficient ways. So also could the worker himself be analysed; the twentieth century has witnessed a great many studies primarily concerned with either breaking the work down into units better suited for human beings, or trying to train the worker to fit in better with the work. The engineering idea dominated both concerns.

Lathes do not, of course, have to be asked their views about being activated or put out to scrap. Workers, unfortunately, some might think, are not lathes. They resent being studied like machines. A great deal of ingenuity has been spent in industrial firms by workers fighting the various systems of work study, a great deal of harm has been committed against nervous people. There is, in fact, evidence that mental strain and stress have been caused by people being asked to perform tasks that have been engineered into such simplicity that they could more easily and more efficiently be performed by morons or highly intelligent animals. Moreover, the hope that engineering would solve all critical organizational problems, although still prevalent, foundered on the fact that some of these problems still remain. Strikes, absenteeism, bad workmanship, poor quality—the organizational problems typical of management concern—have not noticeably dissolved as we have introduced, and vastly improved, our methods of doing work more efficiently.

Part of the trouble, of course, was that the engineering solution had to operate inside the Platonic view. Workers were regarded as simple creatures responding mainly to the two classical stimuli, fear of punishment and promise of reward. But the problems of organizations were not solved. First of all, science and technology have increased their momentum and it has been necessary to increase the amount of know-how on the shop floor. More educated, better-trained personnel are required further down the organization than in the past, and this has created obvious management problems. The army, for example, had been constructed on strict Platonic lines. The shop floor was cannon-fodder, theirs not to reason why. Now that it is necessary to have knowledge of electronics and radar, helicopters and mathematics, shared at the lower levels of the organization, the Army has tried to change its public image and recruit members into a 'professional' organization. The old way of viewing a soldier as a potentially expendable commodity will go, as the costs invested in expensive training increase. New ways of seeing soldiers will have to be created. Secondly, the engineering view was itself challenged between the Wars, as being insufficient to guarantee smooth, conflict-free, high-productivity organizations. Evidence was produced to show, among other things, that workers frequently set their own work targets, irrespective of the management's wishes, that workers do not like their workmates either shirking work or going over a (perhaps unconsciously) agreed level of work performance, that workers frequently react positively to being treated with consideration, that workers also apparently like the opportunity to indicate their views about their working conditions and work methods, and so on—a collection of simple truths that arrived like thunderclaps on the heads of American businessmen and academics involved in the study of industry. If this strikes a reader in the seventies as somewhat extraordinary, it should convince him of how entrenched was the Platonic model, how ingrained were our ways of looking at people in organizations.

The old view was being modified. The workers (for what research *was* going on was still predominantly industrial) were now being exposed to more, and radically different, stimuli—canteens, playing fields, sports clubs, welfare services. Individual bonus schemes were replaced by group bonus schemes. A view of the worker was being advanced that saw him as a gregarious, fun-loving, warm-hearted, affiliative person who, if he could be assured of his place in the work group and in the total organization, would respond by knocking his pan out for the management. A manipulative element could easily be built into these worthwhile new services, and many a manager has appealed to them when confronted by complaints about the conditions or methods of work. "After all we have done for you" is frequently the resigned comment of the benevolent autocrat. No matter how the insight was used, there was now a view of man that competed for as much recognition as the previous one. The previous assumption that personal satisfaction would be achieved through individual efficiency was challenged by another: that personal efficiency would be achieved through individual satisfaction. The wheel had gone half-circle.

By the mid-fifties, a fuller picture of human beings was being drawn up by social psychologists and developed by American management consultants. This was based on a motivational theory that claimed for human beings a hierarchy of needs. Once one level of needs was satisfied, then another level of needs became pressing. The base level was usually survival and security, then social and affiliative needs, then needs of personal esteem; on top of that was a level of needs for autonomy and independence and then ultimately the need for man to self-actualize. The model of man being proposed was that of a being needing to realize all his potentialities, against the demands of our industrial society for obedience, conformity and dependence. Although it received a dressing-up in the fifties, it was the old Renaissance idea of the need to reorganize society to liberate the individual—in fact, this new idea was an old moral philosophical idea of self-realization, brushed up in social psychological jargon.

As an old idea dressed up, it was, however, just as open to the same criticism as its earlier, and much more sophisticated, version. In the first place, the recommendation that we should so organize our organizations that we can actualize people's potentialities does not amount to much. Do we try to actualize all their potentialities? Surely not, for they may be many. Should our potentiality to count be actualized in the statistics division of the company, our potentiality to paint be a reason for a transfer to the paint shop, our potentiality to solve problems open up the options of a number of other departments? And what about our other potentialities—to tell jokes, play the trumpet, cultivate a garden, construct model aircraft, collect stamps? Does the organization play any part in their actualization?

There are traditionally two broad ways of squaring up to the notion of self-actualization. One is to recommend that the individual develops a wide range of potentialities, a *smorgasbord* approach of dabbling here and there, and, in contrast, the second approach would concentrate on one potentiality, what we

F

might call the hedgehog approach. Both, although radically different in their effects, could reasonably be called a pattern of self-actualization. But there are further problems. Some potentialities, if actualized, prevent the development of others. In fact, they may be so exclusive that no other potentiality could ever be developed. Some, however, enhance the development of another. A potentiality for handling statistics would be an asset in a unit concerned with long-range planning.

Trouble is compounded when one moves from an exclusive concern for the individual's self-actualization to an appreciation of the self-actualization of all the people in the organization. It is easy to see that *your* self-actualization, which the theory suggests the organization should be advancing, may be to the detriment of *my* self-actualization. Your skill in statistics may be better than mine, and hence ensure that you are offered the job in the long-range planning unit, which in turn will further your skill even more. Mine will now be thwarted. Or again, my more systematic approach to problems may guarantee me the manager's job and stop your promotion. You cannot, it would seem, have the organization staffed with only actualized chiefs and no non-actualized Red Indians.

One way around this is to maintain that in an organization our individual self-actualizations should be forfeited in the interest of the total self-actualization of all the people in the organization; we should so construct our organization that each of the individual's activities fits into a harmonious pattern and these, in turn, fit into a total, harmonious organizational pattern. But this way will not do either. Do I curb my systematic approach if I am convinced that, in terms of the organization's total plan, it is better that you are offered the manager's job? And who is going to be interpreting the individual's best pattern of self-actualization *and* the fitting of it into the organization's total plan? The job is impossible, and only soluble through double-talk.

The virtue of this Renaissance approach to man is that it draws attention to characteristics of human beings that earlier management theory and organizational behaviour ignored or played down. By claiming for human beings that they are essentially self-actualizing beings, these American psychologists were not so much asserting a psychological theory based on facts as recommending alternative ways of thinking about human beings in organizations. Moreover, if one accepted this view, and developed it within an organization, there was good reason to believe that it would have a pay-off in terms of the individual's interest in his work and also in his productivity. During the sixties and seventies, managers began to think of building difficulties into tasks that would absorb the individual and retain his interest in his job. The old idea of simplifying the job into components that automated equipment or idiots could tackle efficiently was now again being challenged. Human beings were not machines, they were somehow larger than life and we should now be actively engaged in so constructing our organizations that we liberated all the creativity and energy and intelligence that the older models of man had prevented the managers from noticing.

At the time of writing, the self-actualization view of man holds the fort. We ourselves find it unsatisfactory for the reasons which we have just indicated. We feel confident that, as our knowledge of ourselves increases, better models will become available. We want, however, to propose that the best model of man is probably not something that is going to be unfolded in the future but is to be gained from that aspect of human behaviour that has had short shrift from organizational psychologists, namely moral behaviour. We want to propose that the best way to view a human being is, in fact, as a moral being and in the next chapter we argue this at some length. Here, however, we want to conclude this section by reiterating the point that fundamental to our understanding of the behaviour of people in organizations is the role played by the view we hold of what is the essence of a human being.

CHAPTER 6

Morality and Organizations

One of the outstanding characteristics of human beings is their moral behaviour. One of the outstanding characteristics of the modern study of organizations is the inability or reluctance of most of its practitioners to give proper consideration to this fact. Looking through the well-known books of the fifties and sixties on management, administration and organizational behaviour, one will rarely encounter a discussion or examination of the distinctive moral element in the behaviour of an organization's members or of the values propounded by the organization. Generally, it seems, people are only too willing to look at such things as questions about the morality of sexual conduct or of morality and capital punishment, yet shy away from the connections between morality and organizations. This is all the more surprising when one considers that morality is an important regulator of human behaviour. There are other regulators in our society and in our organizations—conventions, customs, etiquette, law, mores—but morality is concerned with critical aspects of people's characters and conduct. Where, for example, moral standards of behaviour conflict with those laid down by convention or law, then they are expected to prevail. When some act is regarded as bad manners, then it is frowned upon, but when it is wrong then it ought not to be done.

We said rarely, for, of course, there have been one or two groups and a few individuals who have raised questions about this subject. For a time in the early sixties there was a debate in the United States about the social and moral responsibilities of businessmen and managers. The argument divided between those who claimed that being a businessman obliged one to take moral responsibility for the health and welfare of employees and for the role of business in the community at large, and others who strongly asserted the propriety of the traditional entrepreneurial role of management. For these latter, the pursuit of profit within free-market-forces happily provided best for the well-being of the community. A number of articles and lectures, and a few books, appeared on the subject during the debate, then sank without trace. Excess profits by armaments firms, the general problem of pollution, the growth of the commercial practice of asset-stripping, and the outcry of indignation at the plight of the thalidomide children, have all contributed towards an awareness that there are problems about the rightness and wrongness of organizational acts, and the moral responsibility of business firms. The Confederation of British Industry set up a working party in 1971 to consider the possibility of creating a practical code of conduct for those who run private industrial firms, with a view to removing, or at least isolating, from industry generally those who practise the worst of the abuses that may be committed within the law. A more radical response to this problem has been that of the Aims of Industry. This organization has sponsored a professional moral philosopher to argue and publicize the case for the profit-motive and uncontrolled-market forces as the guarantors of the good society.

In the American debate a good many of the comments were made within the confines of the Great American Dream. This myth asserts that one can become rich, be important, achieve status in the community, in fact achieve all the good things of life, without upsetting people, or being nasty, cruel or unthinking of others. Indeed, being kind, generous, unselfish and honest are often cited as the necessary conditions for the realizing of fame and riches. Even talent, that quality of the surviving fittest so popular not so long ago, seems to have taken a back seat in the scheme of things. While the myth has now begun to be very ragged around the edges, the machinations of the ad men can still come up with such commercially successful phenomena as the weeny-bopper family pop groups, to tie up some of the fraying ends.

As one writer in the debate claimed, one should endorse the Judaeo-Christian ethic not only because it is right in itself, but also because it pays off in hard cash. A number of popular American television programmes work on this theme, that the good guy will end up better off than the bad guy, that the honest but awkward decision will allow for the reaping of rewards in this life and so on.

The trouble with the Great American Dream is that it has

turned into a nightmare. There are only a few places at the top, and if you are there then someone else is not. Graft, corruption, and double-dealing exist in many organizations. Far from being extolled as a hero of society, the honest person who does stand up against these things may well suffer, mildly perhaps, through lack of merited promotion, or severely, through unemployment. Not inconceivably—for it has happened—there is even the possibility of death as the pay-off for being honest and doing something about it.

Even when regarded as ideological moves to stave off the possibility of governmental controls, or to allay popular disquiet, rather than as honest attempts to change the way things are, the attempts to create codes of conduct for businessmen in the United States were extraordinarily naive. One attempt at a code of conduct proposed that in conflict situations the individual should give priority to, first, the interests of society, second, the interests of his company, and third, his own personal interests. If conflict occurs between your private interests and the company's, let your boss know. If you discover that the company's interests are at odds with the interests of society, let your boss know. Following such a code, businessmen should be able to attempt to make as much money as possible, secured by the knowledge that in doing so this was "the best incentive for the development of a sound, expanding and dynamic society". But the reality is that the difficulties of regulating or even legislating business behaviour with such simplistic guides to action are well-nigh insurmountable. For instance, who should interpret these different interests? How do we establish just what are the individual's private interests, or the company's or even more difficult, those of society? Even if we could agree on these, how should disputes and disagreements between them to be resolved? The most naive aspect of the American debate was the assumption that one could legislate for moral conflict in such a way as to remove it altogether.

The issues were, and remain, much more fundamental, complex and far-ranging than was suggested in the American debate. If a British debate is to be of any consequence it will begin by recognising this, and its corollary, that there are no easy answers. What we want to do is to indicate what we regard as the most important areas that will require clarification and information, if the debate is to be carried on with at least an awareness of the complexity and difficulties of the issues involved.

If we are to begin to identify the important moral problems of organizations and the ways in which they might be tackled, an appropriate language and form of reasoning must be cultivated. Part of our argument in the last chapter was that the study of behaviour in organizations cannot avoid coming up against problems of a moral nature. Even when their perspective is not a moral one, theorists achieve less than they might by using conceptual terms and frameworks which neglect, distort or even deny the distinctively moral aspect of the behaviour of their subject matter. Examples of this abound in the literature on organizations. An organization's goals are sometimes defined in terms of 'society's dominant value-system', when not only is the content of this value-system never specified, but it is also at least arguable that it is a travesty of the facts to assume that a coherent, integrated and popularly agreed-upon set of values exists which adequately defines the relationship between an organization's goals and society. Job satisfaction surveys, for example, which attempt to rank employees' goal priorities with respect to their work, use questionnaires which permit no chance that the surveyed may be able to articulate anything but their 'like' or 'dislike' of their immediate job situation. Again: books on organizational behaviour, if they do consider the moral element, often reduce it to the general notions of emotion and values, and prevent any analysis of behaviour which allows the possibility of treating values and ideals as things rationally acquired and reasonably discussed.

Another example can be seen in the useful distinction between 'instrumental' and 'expressive' behaviour. Instrumental behaviour is behaviour towards an end, rather than an end in itself. Expressive behaviour characterizes actions which are rewarding in themselves, done for their own sake. Yet no consideration is given to the moral implications of describing any behaviour as 'instrumental', let alone a man's complex involvement in an organization. If a man's relation to his job is described as instrumental, this tells us that he works primarily in order to gain a living, asking and getting no other rewards from his employment. But students of organizational behaviour rarely, if at all, then start to investigate the bounds within which men will tolerate acting instrumentally, treating each other as means towards their own private ends, and how they perceive such behaviour. It would seem important, for instance, to know whether or not this was seen to be a necessary but morally undesirable state of affairs, or one which was regarded as more or less right and proper. Categories such as instrumental and expressive have important moral implications, not only for the theorists who use them to describe behaviour, but also for the people themselves. To think that analyses of organizational behaviour can begin and end just by identifying instances of these and relating them to some characteristics of organizational structure, is to do less than justice to the subject matter.

Other instances of such distortions of the moral element in organizational behaviour abound. A person's response to power is described in terms of his cathectic-evaluation orientation. This means that an individual interprets such power in terms of his like or dislike of it, and his understanding of the consequences for him of obeying or disobeying. No room in this analysis is allowed for a situation in which a person may, for instance, *want* to respond positively to another's attempt to control or guide his behaviour, but does not because he also believes that it would not be right for him to do so. If prisons exercise 'coercive' power (that is to say, physical force) then the response of prisoners is described as 'alienative', and no provision is made for the critical fact that it might make a difference if a prisoner regards his fate as legally deserved and morally proper. If this is considered, is it still meaningful to describe his involvement in the prison as being on a par with those who believe that they are victims of police corruption, or an unjust law, or simply innocent and mistakenly imprisoned? Again, as we indicated earlier, some theorists still persist in using a need-fulfilling model of man, which characterizes behaviour in terms of some nebulously defined need-value, so disallowing the possibility of analysing behaviour in terms of the particular and largely socially-derived values that men possess. Self-actualization as a value-characteristic fails to discriminate between the needs of a Greek political prison officer and those unfortunates who inhabit his gaol. Such inadequacy encourages moral insensitivity and makes for bad social science. And even critics fall into the same sort of traps as those they take to task.

An example of this is the case of organization theorists who, critical of the idea that business firms have all the attributes of a happy family with the bonus of money rewards added, often go on, themselves, to define all organizational life purely in terms of power and interests, as if no sense of what was right or wrong could possibly be shared by organizational members and inform their relationships. To study organizational behaviour demands a language which is sensitive to the moral dimension of that behaviour.

This suggests that students of organizations should look carefully at the concepts they already use, for many of these will have, built into them, meanings and implications of a moral nature. Words such as leadership, power, authority, legitimacy, authoritarian, democratic, need, role, norms, consensus and conflict may be adopted for use by the observer of human affairs who claims indifference to, or detachment from, the conditions of his subject matter. No matter the truth or worth of this claim, such an observer cannot hope to escape from the fact that the people he is studying will not share this indifference, for these words will contain the very stuff of the meaning they attach to the situations they are in and the lives they lead. If he wishes to understand them, he must understand these meanings. The language he uses to describe and understand them must not merely accommodate to these meanings, it must allow for moral discriminations that men make with them. Such study ought to be something more than an exercise in applied mathematics. The language must be appropriate in the sense that it is used with an awareness of the moral dimensions of men's behaviour and a sensitivity to the meanings that inform men's moral outlook on the world.

This brings us to the second area of importance. This area concerns the location and clarification of moral organizational problems. It is here that the work of social scientists is essential, to provide the means of mapping and understanding the complexity of the levels at which these problems and situations occur. These problems exist at many levels and in relation to many aspects of the organization. Many problems centre on the face-to-face relationships within organizations. These require an analysis of the situations in which people interact. There are other questions that concern not only those immediately caught up in particular organizations, but larger, more indirectly

connected groups. And there are issues that will involve the
whole community, and which centre on such a question as, what
kind of society ought we to have?—a question that invites the
investigation of the links between the seemingly parochial attributes of organizations and the most wide-reaching political
attributes of the state.

These issues are fundamental. First of all, our own behaviour
is a function of our values. Secondly, organizations, through
their activities, will themselves endorse certain values, and either
explicitly or by implication brand others as irrelevant, unimportant, silly or downright dangerous. Thirdly, society is largely
a conjunction of organizations, and hence the overall shape of
our society will be determined by the types of organizations
that we construct and maintain. It may amplify this point to
recount the story of a Business School where, as a part of a
term's exercise, a group of students were divided into teams,
meeting once a week to tackle a set of problems. The teams were
in competition, simulating rival firms, and the idea of the
exercise was to judge how successful the teams were at the end
of the term. One team started poorly, but after a few weeks, it
picked up and overshot the others, easily finishing well ahead of
them. Some time later, it was discovered that the winning team
had, in fact, realized, after a few weeks, that the other teams
threw their notes and conclusions into the wastepaper buckets.
They had collected these notes, become aware of the business
behaviour of their competitors and had been in an advantageous
position to beat them. This late piece of information occasioned
a debate among the teaching members of the School, some
declaring that, as the students had in fact cheated and obtained
their results by underhand methods, they should be penalised
for the offence and not awarded credits for their performance in
that term's exercise. Others, however, affirmed that the students
had performed exceptionally well and behaved as they would
want them to behave as businessmen hell-bent on maximizing
their opportunities and taking every possible advantage.

The reason for recounting this story is to note the attitudes
of those teaching members who were quite content to applaud
the entrepreneurial activities of their students. For we would
want to say that the behaviour of the students was morally
wrong, that they had broken the rules and hence should be

censured, or, at the very least, certainly not rewarded. To endorse such actions is to ensure their repetition, either in similar exercises inside the Business School or in business behaviour inside firms and companies. The moral question is: would one want to see such action repeated? The answer must be in the negative, on the grounds that to open up such action for moral approval is to undermine the relations upon which life in organizations, and in society, should be built.

The Business School issue was a problem of morality. It was a question about how people behaved and on what grounds they were to be judged for their actions. It also illustrates the importance of recognizing the different views held by different people in organizations, and the kinds of problems that can result from their interaction. The third area of inquiry about morality and organizations would be concerned with establishing the nature of such interactions. There seems to us to be, at least, four major forms of such relationships.

First of all, a member of an organization might be mainly concerned about the way he relates to his workmates and colleagues. He might have a good relationship with them—they work well together, share out the difficult and easy jobs equally, do not tell lies about one another, and do not steal. As this situation might well prevail in most work groups, we might be reluctant under normal conditions to say this was a 'moral' group. Yet if a member joined who behaved in contrary ways, then the appellation might have to be evoked in order to emphasize the immoral behaviour of the outsider. On the whole the members of work groups appear to behave in highly moral ways towards one another; such a description might, in fact, be locked into some definitions of work groups. Again, we would point out in passing that a great deal of social science research on work groups and their behaviour has omitted to examine the moral aspects of that behaviour, or has buried it by the indiscriminate use of terms such as social norms or values.

At another level, there is the relationship between the member of the organization and his superior, or superiors. This is a complex relationship. At the very least, one would expect the superior to ensure that the subordinate knows what is expecte ' of him in the organization and that the subordinate has the right equipment within the right working conditions to fulfil these expectations. It is surprising how rarely in organizations this minimum is attained. Often the disputes and conflicts between a member of an organization and his superior arise when the member feels that his superior has not fulfilled his responsibility and that he, the member, is not being treated as he feels he ought to be treated. The superior often feels that, because he pays the subordinate money for his work, or sanctions the payment of the money, he is entitled to behave in certain autocratic ways, perhaps determined by the history of the organization or by the models of such behaviour prevailing in society at that time. One of the authors witnessed a seaman being reprimanded for leaving the helm of an ore-carrier without saying 'sir'. The reprimander explained that, if you did not enforce the saying of 'sir' at the end of each question or reply, then the 'men' had no respect for you, and anarchy in shipboard relations would result. We read recently of a policeman who was asked to rewrite four times an application form for annual leave which he had erroneously punctuated. The fifth time he wrote out his resignation. From boss to bully is a small step for some.

Another level of relationship is that between the representative of a work group and the manager of the organization. This is the traditional shop steward and manager situation. The role of the shop steward is usually one of bringing to the manager's notice complaints about payments, working conditions and personal injustices. This relationship can be highly-charged because the steward is continually seeking from the manager justice and fair play for the men he is asked to represent. The manager, in his turn, may view the steward as someone who is only concerned with complaining and continually correcting his, the manager's, behaviour. Anyone can be irritated by such a relationship, including the shop steward, who may bring some of the complaints to the manager in the hope that he will reject them as being inappropriate or irrelevant. If a manager concedes to the shop steward's complaints then he may not be acting justly, and hence may lose respect. If the steward refuses to acknowledge that the manager may sometimes have a right to reject his request, then he too will have lost the right to earn respect. The whole notion of respect in industrial relations is complex in its elements and important in its consequences. What goes for the factory floor goes for the classroom, the hospital ward, and the public relations office.

The principal face-to-face relationships in an organization, then, are of a man to his workmates or colleagues, a man to his superior, a man to a subordinate, a man to a worker's representative. We want to maintain that these four relationships are necessarily moral ones, concerning matters of justice, fair play, duties, rights, responsibilities and concerns. Of course, the language in which these relationships are conducted will not necessarily be overtly moral. It is often necessary to study the roles that particular phrases and words play before one can accurately and confidently assert their meanings. To say of a professor, managing director, or hospital superintendent that he is "all right" can, for example, be to report a particular moral evaluation in a very condensed way. But whatever the words used, what is at stake is the amount of respect and the degree of sensitivity that exists among the people of the organization.

This is not simply a question of recruiting saints or graduates from a sensitivity training course into factories, hospitals and universities. In the past, organizations have tried to improve their recruitment along these dimensions, or train their own personnel into better ways of relating to other people. Sometimes industrial firms setting up in an area where industrial relations are poor, may try to screen their employees to avoid recruiting 'trouble-makers'. This policy usually fails, either because the firm so behaves in its own industrial relations as to generate its own indigenous trouble-makers or because the policy of screening has eliminated good leaders and experienced trade unionists whose inclusion might have strengthened industrial relations within the firm. Sometimes firms send their managers on 'human relations' courses, where they might study communications or personnel management or leadership. This has also tended to be a failure within industry, largely because the senior management themselves have no experience of such courses and hence cannot judge the value of any particular one, or because little care has been taken to ensure that the right manager is going on the right course, or because there has been little follow-up to what he has learned once he returns to the organization. Most managers reading this book will know the problem of re-entry well—"what happens when we return to the factory?" Most teachers of management have experienced the sadness of knowing that, even if what they are teaching is prescriptively relevant, it has little hope of being utilized once the manager leaves the lecture room. Such management courses, it is often remarked, are irrelevant for management but valuable for matrimony. One cannot graft on to an organization better ways of behaving as easily as one can in marriage.

It is surprising, however, the lengths to which grafting is taken. In the fifties and sixties, a number of ideas were propounded by various (usually American) authors on methods of management and styles of leadership. It was suggested, for example, that there are four broad styles of leadership—authoritarian, benevolent authoritarian, consultative and participative, or telling, selling, consulting and joining, as one management book translated. Variations of this notion appeared as Theory X and Theory Y, job-centred or employee-centred, work-orientated or human relations-orientated—basic ways in which a manager might relate to his subordinates—and frequently packaged for sale to organizations, as ways in which the improvements in the style of their retrained managers would result in many benefits to the organization. What never seems to have been raised is the question of the moral worth of such managers and their actions.

The failure of methods recruitment, selection and training has been partly due to the crudeness of the techniques, and to our limited understanding of them. More importantly, it is due to the avoidance of fundamental questions about the purposes and structures of organizations, in a society where there is not enough of anything to allow everyone to have their own way—or even a decent and respectable living. It would, for example, be very difficult to envisage relationships of deep mutual respect among scientists engaged together on the preparation of biological weapons of war. If the reply to this is that scientific admiration can allow this to happen, then we ought to be as worried about the state of science as some of the more sensationalist prophets of doom in our society tell us to be. The story has been told of how the wartime production of aeroplanes in the United States was greatly improved when plant workers were shown the planes in operation at airfields, talked to pilots and saw some of the results of bad workmanship. How easily, one wonders, could this kind of response be engendered by organizations whose purpose is to manufacture napalm, or, far less dramatically, body deodorants?

Can we relate the production and sales of plastic Christmas trees to pride in workmanship, loyalty to the firm and a sense of achieving something important? In consideration of these matters it should be remembered that one cannot take at face value the stated aims of the organization. As we pointed out in Chapter Three, one should also look for the amount of resources, expertise and effort actually devoted by organizations towards such ends. An important example of the gap that exists between intent and action is a state mental hospital. How much caring and commitment should be expected from the nurses and orderlies in these hospitals? We said earlier that it would be important to ensure that anyone expected to do a job of work has the right equipment to do it. Our mental hospitals are woefully served in terms of resources and expertise, when the requirements of properly caring for, let alone attempting to cure, their patients are considered. The staff are probably aware that these organizations are, in effect, the institutional carpets under which are swept the doubly underprivileged in our society, the poor and the mentally ill. As public organizations, they stand as monuments to the value the majority of us place on the alleviation of physical misery, the sustenance of human spirit and the shoring-up of human dignity among the most inarticulate and helpless of the adult minorities in our society. For most of us these matters are tolerable because we do not have to live with them, or because there is either ignorance of such things or a feeling that nothing can be done about them. However, for the mental hospital's staff, who are expected to behave adequately in deprived organizational circumstances, the situation must appear desperate at times. Not only are they denied the facilities to do a civilized job, but the priority placed on the care of the mentally-ill is reflected in the low status given to their occupation. Even saints, we suspect, would find it difficult to keep their haloes burnished bright in most of the organizations we maintain for the custodial care of the mentally-ill.

These judgements are related to the purposes of organizations. The goals of an organization can be moral, amoral or immoral. Due to the complexity of goals and the possibility of different goal mixes, these judgements are often difficult to make. This should not stop us making them. Goal analysis, however, helps us to make these judgements on the basis not just of the stated aims of organizations, but on information about the actual mobilization of resources that accompanies the stated intentions. The stated goals of the dominant types of organization in our society constitute a summary check-list of society's values in an altogether more substantial and informative way than do most of the references, in the literature on organizations, to 'society's value-system'. If one could compile such a list, and add to it the actual distribution of the material resources, expertise and personnel devoted to the achievement of these goals, we would have something even more valuable. This would be a weighted hierarchy of goals, a cost-of-living index of the values of our society.

Insight into the complex, but usually unsatisfactory, relationship between the good and the powerful might be achieved if one were to present such an index to the electorate for their own evaluation of how things ought to be in this relationship. Our argument is that the exploration of the moral dimension of living and working within organizations would not only be a valuable social exercise; it would also contribute towards a greater understanding of people's behaviour in organizations. It would give us a greater appreciation than we now have of the moral judgements people make of the goals of the organizations in which they are involved. It would allow us to judge better the validity of a belief widely stated in the organizational literature. This belief usually asserts that people, particularly in industrial organizations, consider organizational purposes and rules on the basis of a pragmatic view of their own self-interest, rather than from a morally-charged perspective. We do not know to what extent this might be the case. Certainly, it is a common opinion. But here again, we would not stop at ascertaining its truth. It would also be important to enquire how people evaluated these purposes and rules. Such moral considerations of the views that people have about the nature and functioning of organizations in our society should be of importance for all who are involved in organization, not least for managers. Those responsible for managing organizations are often in situations from which it is possible to help along or resist the growth of new values. They are, in a sense, the moral custodians of the goals of organizations. Their moral perceptions of the purposes of their organizations will be critical factors in the way in which such purposes are maintained or changed. As an illustration of this, let us recall the university student referred to in Chapter One, who entered university for reasons of individual prudence or perceived social necessity. If many are like him, how will this affect the goals of the university? The authors have certainly listened to many academics and university administrators referring to student expectations in the hushed tones usually reserved for references to the words of Vice Chancellors. If a generalized sanctity is bestowed on all the expectations that students hold on entering university, irrespective of whether they are good or bad, what kind of consequences will follow? Are universities not expected to educate, lead and guide their students? Instrumental behaviour may be all that can be expected of those engaged in the manufacture of plastic Christmas trees. Its intrusion into universities would add greatly to the capability and propensity of our society to produce bigger and better trees. It would at the same time contribute to the amoralising of the goals of the university, to advancing the spread of an instrumental orientation, at the expense of nurturing moral sensibility. Arguments such as this are the beginning, at least, of the sort of practice of moral evaluation which we would hope to encourage in the analysis of organizations. The American debate on the morality of business behaviour failed to lift off the ground because its participants persistently refused to evaluate conscientiously the aims and objectives of the business firm.

Organization structures, too, are important elements of the moral framework of the organization. The four types of face-to-face relations we referred to above are elements in this framework to which general, personal and ethical considerations apply. Organizational goals are the sites marked X, as it were, on a map of the moral territory of organizations, within which such face-to-face relations occur. Organizational structure may be said to represent the dominant pathways leading to these destinations. Perhaps the most persistent and important issue that is raised about such structures concerns the distribution of authority within the organizations that they represent. A political argument that has gone on and off the boil for many years in our society asserts the moral, as against the prudential, value of altering organizational structure, in order to make organizations democratically managed and popularly accountable.

It has been suggested, for example, that worker representatives should join the top management and policy committees of business firms. Experiments along these lines have been legislated for in Yugoslavia and West Germany. These seem to suggest that, while no startling transformations of industrial organizations have been accomplished by such reforms, neither has there been any evidence to suggest the dawn of industrial anarchy. However, the problems about *which* groups should be represented (if any, apart from shareholder representatives and their appointed officials) are difficult. Like most power-sharing schemes, much would depend on the calculations that groups' representatives would make between their own interests and the interests of other, unrepresented groups. How, for instance, would consumer interests be cared for? This question might not seem very important when the consumer is seen as a housewife or an old age pensioner, but what about the consumer beneficiaries of Concorde? The ability to consume is one we all possess, but exercise in ways that are determined in large part by wealth. Such questions reveal just how problematical is the issue of how best to reform the structure of the business firm, and, indeed, most types of organization. The problem of the business firm's structure is one which, in the end, may be seen to be part of the much larger debate between the advantages and disadvantages of a market-orientated, demand economy, as against those of a politically-planned and budgeted economy.

Moreover, from the decentralized, anarchic notion of a managing board populated by some voting for lower prices, others for higher wages and still others for greater profits, one is led to contemplate the idea of an economy centrally ordered by a democratic government arbitrating on behalf of all groups, in the light of some common good. As one solution is achieved— democratic decisions with regard to the creation and distribution of material goods and services, as well as the allocation of personal spending power—another problem is posed, the threat of overwhelming and inefficient public administration spreading throughout society. An introductory text such as this cannot hope to do more than indicate ways in which moral concern raises question after question, the answers to which require the most careful thought, as well as a great deal of inspiration and imagination.

The raising of moral considerations in any discussion on

organizations usually causes discomfort. People generally are not skilled in articulating such issues. Nonetheless, if morality is about what is right and wrong, then behaviour in organizations is largely determined by such considerations. Social scientists in general, and organizational analysts in particular, have not been particularly successful in encouraging the acquisition of such skill. Its encouragement comes from the asking of the right kind of questions. Perhaps of all the groups of contemporary writers on organizations, those who have taken the concept of alienation as a starting point for their inquiries have at least asked some of these questions. Such writers, and to an extent, the theorists who utilize the notion of self-actualization, have identified the deep-seated feeling of entrapment in the sprawling, complex webs spun by organizational bureaucracies, as the malaise of our time. The fact that, to a large extent, men have always felt this way should be taken neither as an excuse for complacency nor as a cause for apathy. Our society provides us with material wealth and comfort on a scale never before achieved, but moral problems will never be rendered irrelevant by material plenty. Our society is often castigated as one in which selfishness, lack of caring and apathy abound. Some critics see it as dominated by competing, well-organized interest groups, each jockeying with the others in some great consumer race. They point out that our political institutions are engrossed in economic issues which ignore or evade questions about social justice. The less well-organized groups—the mentally-sick, the elderly, the disabled—are non-starters in such a race. But is this lack of caring, or selfishness, built into people? It might be more pertinent to ask whether it is due to the fact that people experience a lack of leverage, or influence, in the organizational position where their caring might have an effect. It could be argued, of course, that we live in a democratically organized society in which the vote is the universal currency of leverage on the important decision makers. The sad truth is that even governments appear to find it difficult to achieve their ends. The reasons for this are not absolutely clear. At present we lack a proper understanding of the workings of the complex structure of our organizational society. Organizational and individual purposes accumulate and conflict in a pattern of unintended consequences which seem to thwart attempts at the large-scale management of the social purpose. Some sectional interests in society are well organized for successful goal achievement. Their success is achieved at no small cost to the less well organized. Organizational analysis tempered with moral sensibility could begin to contribute towards the identification and better understanding of those points of leverage at which political and social pressure may be applied towards achieving a better society.

CHAPTER 7

Approaches to Organizational Studies

What we have attempted so far is to indicate the reasons why we think organizations should be studied. We have also indicated what we consider are the important elements in such a study—goals, structure, technology, environment—and the ways in which these elements have helped to order our awareness of the behaviour of people in organizations. What we want to do now is to explore the ways organizations have, in fact, been studied, and to recommend programmes for future study which we consider valuable and important.

The dominant view about the study of organizations might be called the natural science view. With this approach it is proposed that we should collect as many facts as possible about organizations, classify them by some principle or principles, locate their common elements—for example, the properties of technology, size, efficiency, degree of centralization—and identify relationships between these properties. Propositions about these relationships could be expressed as the bases for further hypotheses about organizations, and in this way, a theory of organizations could be constructed, along the same lines as a theory of physics or biology. Such a theory would be as relevant for a small primary school in Wester Ross with twenty pupils and two schoolteachers as it would be for General Motors Corporation, whose sales in 1971 were over eleven billion dollars, for a Communist Party branch in Smolensk and a private psychiatric clinic in California. Just as one can meaningfully assert that most metals expand when heated, so similar supposedly universal propositions could be aimed at in the study of organizations.

Some students of organizations have accepted this view and modelled their activities on what they consider are those of the natural scientists. Impressed with the successes of natural science, they have tended to concentrate their attention on the rigour and precision of their work, on the observable actions of individuals and groups, and on the psychological processes which influence their actions—mainly motives, attitudes and perceptions. Organization theory was to become hard-nosed: data was to be collected with the most rigorous research techniques and propositions were to be asserted in such a way that they could be tested against data which was as quantified as possible. For example, one of the most influential books on organizations, published in 1961, recommended that the comparative study of organizations would "establish the truly universal propositions of organization theory", which builds into the study the very assumptions of the natural science view. The same book proposed, as an important element in the basis of its classification of organizations, a definition of power as "an actor's ability to induce or influence another actor to carry out his directives and any other norms he supports"—one of those definitions of power as helpful as telling us an aunt must have a nephew or niece.

Such hard-nosed organization theory has come to dominate the study of organizations; it has found a place in the literature and in one (at least) of the important social science journals that concerns itself with the study of organizations, the *Administrative Science Quarterly,* published from Cornell University. The current mode of presentation of material in this journal reflects this dominance: the titles of the articles suggest ostensibly scientific enquiry—for example, "The Morphology of Organization", "Organizational Taxonomies", "A Multi-Dimensional Approach Towards a Typology of Bureaucracy", "A Strategic Contingencies' Theory of Intra-organizational Power"—and most of the articles contain statistical tables, almost as if the insertion of tables of figures will provide sufficient props for the prose which, in turn, acts as captions. Some knowledge of statistics has become the sine qua non of the organization theorist, but its uses often obliterate any actual thinking about organizational problems that apparently could not be compressed into the shape of a 5,000-word article.

Taking one of these articles (genuinely at random), we might be better able to see the extent to which accepting the natural science model as being the best way to study organization has led one organization theorist into confusion and error. In December 1965, the *Administrative Science Quarterly* published an article proposing a theory of organization in an axiomatic format. "Eight variables are related to each other in seven simple, two-variable propositions. These seven propositions, with set limits on these propositions and corollaries, complete the theory. It defines two ideal types of organizations. The propositions and corollaries provide twenty-nine hypotheses, which are used to codify a number of research studies and to analyse the problems of organizational change". This is ostensibly scientific. The article went on to claim that a major consideration in the choice of variables was that they were general enough to be applied to any kind of organization. One such variable was complexity, which the author claimed could be equally well applied to an Australian hunting organization, a Roman galley-ship, a Chinese bureaucracy, or an American factory. What we discover about this variable is, as the writer puts it, the greater the number of occupations and the longer the period of training required, the more complex the organization. The variable appears in the seventh proposition: the higher the complexity, the lower the centralization—which, translated in the writer's own language, means that the more occupations there are in the organization and the longer the period of training required, the higher the proportion of occupations whose occupants participate and the more the decisions in which they participate. This, on the face of it, looks unexceptional—the more people there are in the organization, the more the chances are that more people will be involved in decision-making—but, of course, a lot will depend on what we regard as decision-areas, or decision-making, and how we quantify 'higher' and 'lower' and 'the more'.

The same author maintained that it was possible to derive additional hypotheses by applying the simple rules of the syllogism. In one of his examples:

The higher the centralization, the higher the production
The higher the stratification, the higher the production
Therefore: the higher the centralization, the higher the stratification.

This has a plausible, and apparently rigorous, look about it. We are safely in the hands of science. But the exercise is meaningless. First of all, there are no simple rules of the syllogism that deal with the above words. A syllogism is a technical term in logic, referring to a sequence of three and only three terms and of three propositions, each of which must be in a specific logical order.

But here there is no proposition—only a suggested relationship between centralization, production and stratification. Letting p, q and r stand for propositions, one could construct a hypothetical syllogism which is valid:

If p, then q
If q, then r
Therefore: If p, then r

But the author's supposed syllogism is in fact couched in the invalid form of:

If p, then q
If r, then q
Therefore: If p, then r

Substitute for p   That human being is a male student
         for q   That human being has one head
         for r   That human being is a female student

What we have then is the invalid form written out as:

If that human being is a male student, that human being has one head

If that human being is a female student, that human being has one head

Therefore: If that human being is a male student, that human being is a female student.

Secondly, however, it is difficult to see how the author could turn these apparently scientific propositions into propositional form. "The higher the centralization, the higher the production" suggests a causal relationship, that, as a matter of fact, *because* there are fewer jobs whose occupants participate, the more units of production are produced and the greater the rate of increase. This is obviously nonsense. Even if we try his new conclusion "the higher the centralization, the higher the stratification", this comes, in his language, to: the fewer the proportion of occupations whose occupants participate in decision-making, the more there is in the difference in rewards between jobs and the relative rates of mobility between them. It is difficult to make much of this. It looks, in fact, as if the author has derived a nonsense correlation from unclear premises.

We have remained with this example not because it is an exception to the general run of such articles, but because it amply illustrates the results of being over-impressed with the natural science approach. This particular article was criticized in later numbers of the journal, but the point of view which generated such nonsense still pervades organizational studies.

Recently, there have emerged criticisms of this dominant view. Some philosophers of science have objected to the abstract nature of the earlier account, as well as the apparent constraints of symbolic logic. Most of all, they have objected to the earlier account's lack of interest in actual scientific procedures. Studying scientific activities and the history of science reveals that the language of science is not aseptic, for its terms are loaded with the scientific theory in which they are used. To understand what the terms mean, we must learn the theory. The natural science model, in other words, which has been so dominant, has been wrongly constructed; our descriptions of the scientific process, the way we see the role of theory and hypothesis are all wrong. Science itself, it has turned out, is not so simple nor uniform as was earlier assumed to be the case.

There appears to be no consensus now about the nature of scientific theory and scientific method, about the problems of prediction and explanation. How do we distinguish between crystal-ball gazing and prediction? Why do we accept the complex notion that the construction of the Pyramids was planned, pro-grammed, staffed, co-ordinated and supervised by a group of Egyptian priests, rather than the simpler explanation that a technologically superior race from somewhere near Barnard's Star arrived and put them together one morning? Why do we believe some general statements to be laws—"all organizations tend to have communication problems"—while denying this status to other general statements—"all paperback books tend to be cheaper than hardback ones"? Is scientific proof to mean proof as in physics, or in biology, or in sociology, or in the eating of the pudding? Or are there some common elements to all of these proofs?

A second set of criticisms has rejected the view that social science (of which the study of organizations would be a part) is really only natural science writ, for the moment, rather small, or not yet developed on the same scale as natural science, and that there is no difference in principle between the two activities. The study of organizations, like all the other social sciences, should not be awaiting its Newton or Darwin to make sense out of the thousands of facts about organizations that we have at hand. It would be like waiting for Godot. Rather, they have maintained that social science is radically different from natural science, some of these critics going so far as to assert that the whole idea of a science of man is untenable. Social science should be more appropriately termed social studies, a heterogeneous collection of inquiries, as one writer put it, strung together on the common theme of human action. Anthropology becomes travellers' tales, psycho-analysis a collection of more or less informed hunches, economics a series of reflections designed to bring into focus a new way of carrying on economic practices.

A third set of criticisms of the natural science view has come from within the study of organizations itself. Some students of organizations have questioned the whole approach towards a theory of organization. To try to establish a broad, conceptual framework about organizations that could be equally relevant to, as one of them put it, Imperial Chemical Industries, the Catholic Church, and the Parks and Gardens Department of the Leeds City Council, was not likely to result in a significant increase in the volume of useful knowledge at our disposal. As another observer put it, it is like looking at rugby football, netball and cricket and concocting a theory about all ball games. There would not appear to be much point in such an exercise, even assuming that such a theory could in fact be constructed.

Although these criticisms have originated from different interests and, in fact, there is little evidence that the protagonists are aware of one another, there is now increasing realization that we cannot easily build a science of organization by deciding to go out into the world and collect a number of facts, classify them, prepare hypotheses about these facts and create a theory on the successful hypotheses. At the first stage, we are stopped by the difficulty of being sure of what a fact actually is. It is not sufficient to indicate that facts are what is out there, data which we simply record. What we need is a conceptual framework to organize our experiences of this so-called data; we need a language in which to record the data, but the language itself dictates perception of the data. If you like, we approach the world with some preconceptions of what it is we are looking for; these preconceptions organize the data into facts. To put it yet another way, it is not the case that we first collect a lot of facts and then incorporate them into concepts. The process is much more interactional, concepts informing us what will constitute a fact, and the facts redefining the concepts. We cannot understand what a 'chairman' or 'shop steward' is, without also knowing what it is for someone to be a chairman or shop steward, without, that is, having the concept of chairman or shop steward. We need to know not only the formal definition of a chairman or shop steward, but also to be able to recognize examples of chairmen and shop stewards when we observe them.

The issue, then, may not be so much about the facts that we collect or organize or present in argument or debate, as about the concepts that we employ to organize the facts. Perhaps this can be most easily seen in the concepts that are used to define an organization. Some writers have taken an organization to be a system of relations between people, in which the interactional behaviour of the people is the common factor uniting technology, structure and personality. Others have seen the distinctive characteristic of an organization to be that it is formally established for the purpose of achieving certain goals. Another has seen it as a system of consciously co-ordinated activities or forces of two or more persons. Another has defined it as the ordered mobilization, control and manipulation of people for certain ends. And so on. The point is that each one of these definitions has a persuasive look about it, attracting us towards some feature of organization that, in the judgement of the writer, is considered to be paramount and overriding. Yet interactional behaviour, goal achievement, conscious co-ordination, ordered mobilization, makes one suspect that it is not a case of blind men describing different parts of an elephant, but that the blind men are describing different elephants—or crocodiles, eagles and sharks.

This is not to maintain that one cannot have any facts at all about organizations. That would not be true. One can easily produce singular statements of fact—Upper Clyde Shipbuilders went bankrupt in 1970. Or dispositional statements—the Chairman of the Board is keen on innovation. Or comparisons—the sales of Standard Oil are less than those of General Motors. Or general—there is more joint consultation in British engineering companies than American ones. These are all examples of possible facts. There may be difficulties about their truth or falsity, due to the availability of evidence, or ambiguity and vagueness of the terms used, but the procedures for resolving such difficulties are not too complex. It is doubtful, however, if these facts, in the old phrase, speak for themselves. They are only picked out and used and take on significance by the prior decision of the organization theorist, or anyone else interested in such facts. The theorist gives them houseroom in his analysis. All facts are selective, because it is human beings who select them.

Because of this, some writers have gone on to maintain that all statements in social science are value-laden, and that to remove the value-elements in such statements would be to radically alter their meaning. 'Mother' might be used in some statement as a fact of biology and kinship relations, but in our society it would have to be specially qualified to erase suggestions of responsibility and care. It has even been argued that to assert that Smith is Chairman of the Board of Directors, which appears, on the face of it, as a simple fact describing the post that Smith has in the company, is to imply that Smith has certain rights and obligations, since these are locked into the meaning of 'Chairman of the Board'. Of course, to imply that Smith has rights and obligations is to make a statement that has value-content. This is the stuff of social science; trying to render the value out of such statements is to render them valueless, or downright weird. How could one describe the workings of a concentration camp, without employing value words? If this was a serious request— for example, to a team of management consultants invited to suggest more efficient methods in the camp—then it would not be a request to tidy up our value-laden words, to reform our language. It would be a request that itself would imply a change in our view about human beings and the way they relate to one another. It would also be a monstrous request.

We might not want to go so far as to suggest that it is not possible to obtain non-value-laden statements. We have just noted that facts as such are available to the student of organizations. But we would want to acknowledge that in observing organizations, we observe efficient or inefficient, effective or ineffective, autocratic or consultative, mean or generous, sycophantic or outspoken behaviour. We are involved in value-judgements, but they are none the less descriptive. The behaviour is not, first of all, observed and then evaluated; our values, in fact, allow us to describe the behaviour. So, for example, when we define an organization in terms of power, we are already on a course of investigation that will tend to ensure the omission of certain elements of the organization and the distortion of others. As we pointed out earlier, if all power relations cover friendship, affection, advice, influence, guidance, approval, admonition, and so on, then the definition is itself of dubious value. If it is so used as to exclude possibilities of relating to human beings that are not modelled on the gangster with a gun in your back, then the claim is just false.

If, as we have just seen, there is disagreement about how the unit of analysis, the organization, is to be defined, then we would expect even more disagreement over the nature of organization theory. This expectation is not disappointed. Although there is a general increase in the literature on the theories of organization, there is no sign of cohesion in the field, except in the eyes of those who back or propound one particular theory and hence will asume that, if their theory is among this general increase, it must therefore be in the ascendancy. Some have seen it as referring to all kinds of studies of formal organizations, others as a set of propositions stemming from a definable field of study which can be termed organization science. Others again see it as being on the periphery of general systems theory, although the concept of a system itself ranges in meaning from any set of two or more variables and one or more rules of interaction, to a relationship which has a supply of resources (the input), a conversion process (the throughput), and a production of objects (the output). Others, yet again, see it as an amalgam of studies—as a branch of sociology studying the social structure of organizations, as a branch of social psychology studying the behaviour of individuals or groups as members of organizations, as a branch of political theory studying power relations and methods of control in organizations.

One might expect a certain degree of confusion about a subject that is relatively new in the scheme of social science but there is the additional point to be made that similar confusions about the nature of organization theory also prevail in the older social sciences that are referred to as the 'real' basis for the study of organizations. There has been raging within the study of politics, for example, an apparently three-cornered struggle between philosophy, theory and science, over the nature of the subject. The decline and death of political theory were regularly reported during the ascendancy of those political scientists impressed with the successes of natural science. Certainly, at the moment, it would be fair to assert that there is no subject of politics unified in terms of concepts, theories or methods. Sometimes, of course, the old political theorists and the new political scientists were asking different kinds of questions. The old ones had raised questions, for example, about the nature of the state and of political obedience, whereas the new ones were interested in political socialization and voting behaviour. But, on the whole, the new ways have not yet produced the expected theories with strong explanatory capacity, and the old questions are still around. Some of the Americans who avoided the draft for the Vietnam war must have asked questions about the nature of political obedience and about the legitimate powers of the state. Our point here, however, is that the kind of intellectual disarray apparent in the study of organization can also be seen within the more established study of politics.

It is a consolation of a sort to know that the study of organization is not alone in being a subject of disagreement. The fact is that politics and all the other social sciences are in the same boat, mainly, as we pointed out earlier, because of these deep-seated disagreements about the nature of science and social science. But this is not a cause for despair. We should recognise the elements in this debate and try to assess their different merits, for, at the end of the day, it will likely turn out that, as in most philosophical disputes, there will be points of value on all sides. We would not wish to explore these issues in an introductory book, but rather conclude this chapter with some final points that would bear upon such an exploration. First of all, we should realize that social inquiries—and hence the rise and development of social sciences— are usually the result of particular concerns, problems and difficulties. We want to know, for example, what factors would help the Indian economy, whether hanging is a deterrent for would-be murderers, or if old-age pensions can be increased. In the field of organization studies, we are generally interested in the one organization or organizational sub-unit. We want to know of the problems of voluntary organizations such as Oxfam. We want to know about the organization of the University of Stirling during the winter of 1972/73, when it experienced student disaffection and unrest. We want to know about London

Weekend Television, the U.N. Security Council and Unilever.

Secondly, such social inquiries cannot easily be placed within the total province of one social science, but often depend for their full analysis on a number of social disciplines. God, as someone once remarked, did not divide the world into social science departments, but neither did He ensure that these departments always housed the same type of person or activity. One often finds social scientists within a single discipline pursuing different activities; and in different disciplines, engaged in similar work or work with overlapping concerns. There is no doubt, for instance, that the traditional concerns of political theory—the nature of rights, power, authority, equality, leadership, obedience, decision-making—are directly relevant to students of organizations. It would be a mistake, however, to go on and claim that the study of organizations is really political theory, for similar connections of relevance could have been culled from anthropology, economics, sociology and psychology. The study of organizations, we would readily agree, is an inter-disciplinary activity, but mainly because all social sciences must be inter-disciplinary.

Finally, we should recognize that we need all the help we can obtain. This means not only being alert to work being done in related social sciences, but also being sensitive to the insights and descriptions of the artists in our society. Just as we lose much of the information content of speech by printing it, so we often lose much of organizational life in the records of academics. We often recommend our student to Joseph Heller's *Catch 22*, as essential reading for those concerned with the workings of modern organizations. We would strongly urge the importance of those aspects of our minority and popular culture that deal with organizational affairs, for there we have provided for us an abundance of serious and comic comment on the problems, foibles and rewards of life in organizations. It must surely be one of the most suspect features of contemporary social science that it has had neither the inclination nor the structure to relate to and draw upon the culture of our time.

CHAPTER 8

Conclusion—A Case in Point

We said in the last chapter that it was usually particular concerns, problems, and difficulties that prompted social inquiries. This is why the case-study as a method of study has provided the most interesting information about organizations. In fact, most attempts to construct theories of organization have been based on the findings of studies of particular organizations. What we want to do now in this final chapter is to draw together some of the main points of the earlier chapters. This purpose, we feel, can be most satisfactorily served through the examination of a genuine issue—in this case, the problems of the theatres in this country which are subsidized by the Arts Council. There are four reasons why we have chosen this example to illustrate our final chapter. One: as we mentioned earlier, the study of organization is heavily informed by studies of industrial and commercial firms, but we have also implied throughout the book that such a study has relevance for the non-industrial world. Two: subsidized theatres are organizations which we jointly researched several years ago and since then we have retained an interest in their activities, in particular those of the Glasgow Citizens' Theatre. Three: the theatre has the advantage of being essentially concerned with the organization of creativity. As such, it provides an interesting contrast to the type of bureaucratic organization maintained by the majority of organization theorists to have outlived its usefulness. The organizations of the future will approach the problems of integrating the needs of the individual and the organization's goals, of the distribution of power, of the control of conflict, of responding appropriately to environmental changes, achieving consensus and commitment in ways that will differ radically from bureaucratic solutions. For example, in the control of conflict, the bureaucratic organization looks to its higher administrative and managerial levels to resolve difficulties between ranks, whereas the new organizations will be more specialized and professionalized and have an increased need for interdependence and the sharing of leadership. Largely ignored by organization theorists, the theatre, however, has some non-bureaucratic features that we consider will be worthwhile studying as we make the transition from the old to the new style organizations. Four: our comments bear upon the difficulties of providing subsidized cultural activities to local communities, a matter which, we expect, will be the concern of many people interested in the provision of such performances for their own sake. These difficulties are to do with the political questions of what is best for a community and how this ought to be provided. Debate about the role of the subsidized theatre combines elements of an aesthetic, political and administrative nature.

Arts Council subsidized theatres are a sub-class of theatre organizations. They are theatres, all or part of whose revenue comes in the form of grants and guarantees from the Government-sponsored and financed Arts Council of Great Britain. They are sometimes called non-commercial theatres, presumably because their subsidies insulate them from the free market imperative of covering their costs through the sale of their product on the open market. This fact alone has various implications, two important ones being that the prices they charge need not be sufficiently high for them to cover their costs, and that the types of plays they produce need not be chosen exclusively on their assumed attraction of large audiences. Commercial pressures are thus eased, but other pressures take their place. The theatres must acknowledge the conditions under which subsidies are granted. Although the Arts Council is frequently claimed to be committed to a policy of non-interference in the affairs of the various theatres it subsidizes, this is no more than a formal goal, retained for obvious ideological reasons. In the nature of things, the Arts Council can and does interfere with local autonomies, and the criteria by which it continues to supply grants to particular theatres and the reasons it puts forward for stopping such a supply are factors which any particular theatre must always take into account. No adequate organizational picture of a particular subsidized theatre can be presented without a close examination of the workings of the Arts Council.

The provision of 'good drama' or 'the best drama available'

H

are the usual goals for which the subsidized theatres are said to exist. Sometimes these goals are made more specific, and it is claimed that such theatres exist to provide the best drama 'at prices which all will be able to afford'. Or again: a number of these theatres have made special provision for children and present educational programmes intended to encourage a greater interest and involvement in theatre among young people. It will be readily seen that difficulties can arise in the interpretation of what constitutes 'good theatre' or 'best drama'. Is this the provision of established classics? Is it new experimental theatre that cannot find a place in the commercial theatres? Is it middle-range entertainment? One Arts Council spokesman suggested that it might be a comforting mixture of all of these, when he stressed that a necessary condition for the provision of a subsidy to a theatre was that it provided what he called "a broad repertoire of drama". Another spokesman created a controversy of no small dimensions when he complained that theatres had interpreted Arts Council policy too literally as support for non-popular drama.

Difficulties over the interpretation of the aims of such theatres are compounded by their organization structures. Formal administrative authority is customarily vested in Boards of Management, which bear some resemblance to the legal and formal structure of limited companies, with the Board being responsible to a small and privately selected group of shareholders. Such persons very often play two roles at once in relation to the theatre, one as shareholders, the other as directors on the Board. In such cases, the practical answer to the important question as to whom the Board is responsible is that it is responsible to itself and only in a fictional sense to an outside and publicly constituted body of people. Such Boards persist as self-appointed and non-accountable bodies of part-time members who will give a limited amount of their attention and a limited part of their working lives, to the affairs of the theatre with which they are associated. The main advantage of such a Board is that it can be composed of independent people of different abilities, who might take a more objective view of the theatre than the professional producers, actors and other workers. The main disadvantage is that the people who are responsible for the formation of the theatre's policies are not usually responsible for their execution; most people are going to be more careful and precise about formulating policies when they know they are going to have to carry them out.

Under the Board will be the usual positions of artistic director, administrator, producer, designer, front-of-house manager, who will usually be younger people than Board members and come from different social backgrounds. But the probable differences of social background and age recede before the main difference of orientation, for the professional staff are likely to be making decisions according to a set of criteria which could easily differ from those that underly the collective judgements of the Board. Conflict between the part-time 'men of repute'—local citizens of good renown—and the full-time 'members of the theatre', who see their first loyalty to the theatre and their fellow professionals, will be quite accepted. Such conflicts, in fact, have been the main feature of the structural arrangements for such theatres; during the fifties and sixties instances reached the pages of the national press. Sometimes, however, the disputants were not well enough known; sometimes, they were reluctant to wash such dirty linen (as it would be interpreted) in public; sometimes, they were concerned with trying to avoid being labelled troublemakers and thus jeopardizing their careers within the prevailing system of theatre structures. Frequently, of course, such conflicts were described as instances of 'ordinary human relations', merely 'personality clashes', but we would suggest that such an analysis is too easy and unsatisfactory, and that, in fact, built into the structure were ingredients that would make relationships, at the best, difficult and demanding and, at the worst, inflammatory and hostile.

This problem is never, of course, seen in such organizational terms as we have been discussing throughout this book. It is usually posed in the different form of—how much freedom should the artistic director actually have in a theatre? Some believe that the full-time director should have complete and absolute licence in the choosing of plays and the managing of all that goes on within the theatre. Others feel that theatre boards should decide the broad criteria according to which a programme of plays should be chosen, and also that boards should reserve the right to have the final say as to whether a particular play should be produced or not. Still others hedge their bets and advance views that look 'right', but which on closer examination can be shown to be vague enough to justify almost any administrative set-up in the theatre. The issue could be more profitably looked upon as the problem of how best to administer a creative organization. From this angle, we can see that this problem is not unique to the theatre. It is one which besets television stations, newspaper companies, publishing houses, research organizations and universities.

When we turn to possible technological and economic influences on subsidized theatres, we can appreciate further anomalies. Technical development in the theatre has been marginal in relation to production, in basic costs. While they have resulted in different presentations of drama, technical changes have not resulted in productivity changes which might reduce unit costs. Putting on a Shakespeare play still requires the same number of actors as when the play was first written. Meantime, salaries have risen, the costs of building, heating, costumes and administration have all increased. A gap appears between possible income from box office and necessary costs of production. But this analysis is only valid if one accepts that the theatre will never benefit economically from technical innovations and that people will be unlikely to pay economic prices for their tickets. The first assumption may be untenable in an age of cinema and television, both instances of technical developments in communications and both proven vehicles for the presentation of dramatic art. Perhaps the new forms of theatre—theatre-in-the-round, intimate close theatre, apron-stage theatre—will have implications for the economics of the subsidized theatres. The second assumption again is only tenable if we accept without question that the availability of theatre of the present sort, at the present level of numbers, and at the present level of prices, is an unquestionable good.

Probing the factors of technology and economics brings us back to the policies and activities of the Arts Council. The arguments in favour of subsidy, central to the activities of the Arts Council, are usually asserted in terms of the self-evident goodness and richness of the live performing arts and the necessity in a civilized and democratic society to allow such good things to be available to all, at a price all can afford. But this argument itself is not self-evident. For a start, the almost exclusive beneficiaries of twenty-five years of subsidized theatre are the well-educated and the well-off. The few surveys of theatre audiences that have been made in these theatres have shown that the patronage of the theatre comes from a rather well-defined and extremely narrow section of the population. Moreover, despite the subsidy, these theatres are not all that popular, which would suggest that they are not providing the art that most people consider attractive or meaningful. One could ask if the fact of subsidy has not insulated the theatre from a potentially broader section of the population. Being in a position to tolerate a certain number of empty seats, those who exercise control over theatre policy may become too rigid and narrow in their interpretation of live drama. It may well be that we have at present a situation in which the few have their narrow and conventional tastes subsidized at the expense of the many who could be enjoying more meaningful drama. Moreover, there is evidence that the Arts Council has been extremely reluctant to finance many cultural activities that do not fit easily within the acceptable range of middle-class culture. Jazz, cinema and science fiction, for example, would be examples of such art forms.

How would we judge the effectiveness of subsidized theatres? The Arts Council's problem of which theatres to support, and by what sums of money, can only be satisfactorily solved if an organizational concept of effectiveness is established. By 'effectiveness' one usually refers to the extent to which the real goals of the organization are actually attained. In the theatre this must be a complex built up from an analysis of a variety of factors. One of these would try to assess the quality of the individual plays— not an easy task, particularly when the work of modern playwrights is being considered. Another would judge the ways in which individual plays are balanced in a season's programme, for this is often the way the distinctive character of a theatre is determined. Another would be concerned with the quality of the actual productions, for this will also contribute to the effectiveness of the theatre. Directive interpretation, acting standards, stage and costume design, stage management and lighting will all add up to, or detract from, the quality of the final product. Another factor would be the actual audience attendances, usually the most visible and easiest-to-measure indicator of organizational effectiveness in the theatre. In the case of the subsidized theatres, however, there are snags about this particular factor. They are not given money to put on plays that are 'popular'. A high level of attendance might threaten the size of the grant from the Arts Council. On the other hand, it seems reasonable to assume that a theatre that plays to empty auditoria is totally ineffective. The factor of audience becomes in turn related to the type of play and the repertoire of the theatre, its pricing policy, seating capacity and running costs, as well as the age and class distribution of those who compose the audience. Nor does this exhaust the range of factors that should be considered about the effectiveness of the theatre. There are many others—for example, the overall economic viability of the organization, the degree of effort it has to engage in to maintain its necessary income from whatever sources, and perhaps the effectiveness of the theatre as the provider of a variety of the arts and not just live drama.

The previous section dealt in summary fashion with some of the problems that beset the theatres of this country that are regularly financed from the Arts Council, and demonstrated some of the perspectives from which a student of organizations would look at an organization. As we have mentioned earlier, the student is often presented with a problem. In the case of the subsidized theatres, an analysis might have been prepared as a response to a number of questions. For example, does this theatre have an identifiable product? Do we know what sort of audience would want this product? Are our expectations about the present audiences being met? Should we change the policy—or market the product more vigorously and discriminately? Is the pricing policy realistic? Too often in the past, we have been provided with fashionable analyses which nonetheless turn out in practice to be wide of the mark. To reduce the management-director conflicts to matters of personality clash, for example, would set us off on errands of management and director selection or even, perhaps, psychological testing, but would not substantially alter the factors in the situation that encourage such clashes of personality.

Among many students of theatre now, it has become conventional wisdom that the villains of the piece are oligarchic boards. The cry has gone out for making boards "more democratic", but not many have bothered to ask "democratic to whom?". Few have pleaded for such theatres to be responsible to democratically elected local authorities, even fewer have entertained the notion that the cry "democracy" may be taken up within the theatre itself. Similarly, to assume that the provision of 'legitimate theatre' is a clear-cut overall objective for subsidized theatres, is again to ignore the complexity of the theatre's environment and structure, which will ensure various and varied interpretations of this organizational goal.

During our research into theatre organizations it was difficult to avoid encountering moral issues. We found one group of actors experimenting with a democratic form of play-direction. Some of them would have wished to extend the idea to the management of the theatre as a whole. In one theatre a great deal of conflict occurred between successive directors and the Board of Management. Much of it stemmed from moral disagreements about how relationships ought to be conducted. Often controversy over plays had to do with the moral nature of their contents. In some theatres, board members have failed to commit themselves wholeheartedly to the affairs of the theatre because they lacked tolerance towards the idiosyncratic life-styles of people in the theatre. We have witnessed encounters between people which were charged with moral concern—a director 'retiring' a leading player just before opening night because he was not up to the part, and trying to do it in the way that would cause least hurt to the actor. Or a chief designer sacking an assistant who designed brilliantly, but behaved badly.

One final point. We explained at the beginning of this chapter why we selected the subsidized theatre as our final example. We would want our reader to consider his own organization in a similar fashion. It may be that, as he has gone through the book with us, he has been reviewing his own organizational experience in a new light. We can be sure that we shall not have met with all his problems in this introductory text. It is unlikely that they could be met in several other volumes. Human life in organizations fortunately still evades all the categories of the human sciences. But such an investigation by the reader will be a process of education.

We can perhaps usefully classify the skills of education into four sets. First of all, there are the relatively straightforward technical skills which, when acquired, enable people to cope with an identifiable set of problems through the application of certain procedures, methods and techniques. Doctors, engineers, welders, airline pilots, accountants are all examples of people in occupational roles who have acquired a set of technical skills for coping with recognizable and more or less predictable, recurring problems. Secondly, there are the intellectual skills of thinking analytically, grasping abstract notions and relationships. They are not usually identifiable with any particular set of problems. Thirdly, there are social skills. People vary in their ability to relate to people, to create and sustain deep and lasting relationships. Such skills are usually acquired by countless demonstrations and experiences of being with other people. Conceivably a man shipwrecked on a desert island may acquire certain technical skills. He could read technical manuals and programmed-learning courses, carry out practical investigations. He could also develop his ability to think. But it is difficult to imagine him adding to his social skills through such means. Lastly, there are human skills based on moral values about human beings. Respect for persons, consideration for others, a belief in the sanctity of human life, trust, and respect for truth, are examples of such values. Social skills can be distinguished from human skills, as the former can be acquired and practised without regard for other people, except as means for some immoral end. Such use of social skills would be regarded as manipulative because it does not stem from a respect for persons. A salesman who successfully cultivates social skills to sell more of his wares will be a good salesman, but not necessarily a good person. The very notion of 'skills' is itself dubious, when it refers to the ability to relate to other people in a moral fashion, yet it is not an absolutely impermissible term, for it does suggest that better ways of relating to others may be acquired for the right reasons.

The study of organizations obviously requires the teaching of intellectual skills, and in an earlier chapter we argued for the inclusion of a moral perspective. The prudential needs have prompted the study of organizations as a means of producing improved, supposedly scientific methods of handling and relating to people. A major part of the literature contains the fruits of such endeavours. Yet there has not emerged from such work a body of techniques which will turn a trainee manager into a competent one. No straightforward body of techniques will provide a person with the means of becoming a competent manager.

If that were the case, it would be in a world in which all values coincided and there was no disagreement about what we should be doing, or where conflict did not matter to those who manage, because their activity excluded a respect for people.

In our present society, it would seem to us that working in organizations is a relational, social activity, best served by good education, not technical training. What we would require, for example, of people who become managers, is that they have a good education and that they are good persons. Any management training which fails to incorporate a proper intellectual analysis and appraisal of the organizational situations in which managers act and a consideration of the moral dimensions of organizational life, will be seriously deficient. This is not to claim that the values that people hold must needs be of one kind, only that they are held for good reasons and with an awareness of the values of others. Our satisfaction in this book will rest not only on the possibility of illuminating people's experiences in organizations, but also on the hope of vindicating the moral lives of people in organizations.

Suggestions for Further Reading

A. *General Texts*
1. March, J. G. (ed), *Handbook of Organisations,* New York, Rand McNally (1965). An expensive and large book of readings. Its contents are illustrative of the variety of perspectives and problems that are prompted by the study of organizations. It contains surveys (by recognized specialists in the field) of the literature on particular types of organizations.
2. Etzioni, A. (ed), *A Sociological Reader on Complex Organizations,* (2nd edition), New York, Holt, Rinehart and Winston (1970). This is a well-chosen collection of readings by a well-known theorist and anthologist. It is organized into sections on particular aspects of organizations.

B. *Case Studies*
1. Crozier, M., *The Bureaucratic Phenomenon.* Tavistock Publications (1964).
   Crozier is a French sociologist. One of the many merits of this depth study of the workings of particular state bureaucracies is the skill with which he relates organizational matters to features of French society.
2. Gouldner, A. W., *Patterns of Industrial Bureaucracy,* Routledge and Kegan Paul, (1955). This study draws on and elaborates a particular theoretical perspective on organizations.
3. Selznick, P., *TVA and the Grass Roots,* Berkeley and Los Angeles; University of California Press (1949). As we indicated in chapter two, this case study pays particular examination to the competing demands of bureaucracy and democracy.

C. *The Philosophy of Social Science*
   1. Ryan, A., *Philosophy of Social Science,* McMillan (1970).
       A competent and modern introduction to the philo-
       sophical problems and issues of social science.

D. *Moral Philosophy*
   Hudson, W. D., *Modern Moral Philosophy,* McMillan
   (1970). One of the many very good introductory texts in
   this field.